The
Top 40
Traditions
of
Christmas

The
Top 40
Traditions
of
Christmas

The Story Behind the Nativity, Candy Canes,
Caroling, and All Things Christmas

David McLaughlan

BARBOUR
PUBLISHING

© 2012 by Barbour Publishing, Inc.

Print ISBN 978-1-61626-860-2

eBook Editions:
Adobe Digital Edition (.epub) 978-1-62029-108-5
Kindle and MobiPocket Edition (.prc) 978-1-62029-109-2

All scripture quotations are taken from the King James Version of the Bible.

Published by Barbour Publishing, Inc., P.O. Box 719, Uhrichsville, Ohio 44683, www.barbourbooks.com

Our mission is to publish and distribute inspirational products offering exceptional value and biblical encouragement to the masses.

ecpa Member of the
Evangelical Christian
Publishers Association

Printed in the United States of America.

Contents

Introduction

Welcome to
*The Top 40
Traditions of Christmas!*

Christmas traditions form the foundation of the holiday season—and this book considers the "story behind the story" for forty favorite customs.

Familiar things like Christmas trees, candy canes, Santa Claus, and lighting displays have little-known histories or deeper meanings that make them worthy of contemplation for those of us who celebrate Christmas as the birth of Jesus Christ, the Son of God.

The Top 40 Traditions of Christmas provides that intriguing information for the most beloved songs, movies, characters, and activities of the season. We hope you enjoy the readings that follow.

And, by the way, Merry Christmas!

1
Advent Calendars

Who?

Early Advent calendars were homemade affairs costing nothing but time and imagination. With the increasing popularity of the tradition, inevitably someone would commercialize it. Hand-drawn calendars were in use as far back as 1851, but the first printed version was made by Munich printer Gerhard Lang in 1908. It came with twenty-four little pictures that could be fixed to the cardboard background. It took several years for the idea of covering the backboard with twenty-four little doors to be introduced.

Lang's printing company went out of business twenty years later, but his idea survived and is now a popular part of the Christmas tradition.

What?

The first Advent calendars were simply ways of marking the passing days in the run-up to Christmas. People made chalk marks on their door in excited anticipation of the day the Christ child would come through it.

Gerhard Lang's mother stuck sweet treats to a cardboard calendar each morning before he woke. The modern equivalent, which she inspired and he developed, has little boxes with chocolate figures waiting to be uncovered.

Some Advent calendars still have Christmas or faith-oriented scenes behind the chocolate treat, but, in a more secular age, they are often simply images of general celebration or pictures of the celebrities or animated characters endorsing the calendar.

Where?

Like many other Christmas traditions, the Advent calendar was a German invention. It is thought to have originated among Lutheran communities and spread to other churches in the area, but the tradition remained in Germany until the outbreak of World War II. Production of Advent calendars ceased during the war years. Afterward a German manufacturer reintroduced the Advent calendar to the world and helped make it an important part of the modern Christmas.

These days Advent calendars are sold and displayed in most countries where Christmas is celebrated. Being displayed by children from the first day of December, they are the first sign of Christmas in many households.

When?

The Advent season begins on the fourth Sunday before Christmas and ends on Christmas Day. Modern Advent calendars usually begin on the first day of December, with a compartment for that day and each of the next twenty-four. Perhaps in an effort to outsell their competitors, some manufacturers add an extra day for Boxing Day. Some even go as far as New Year's Eve. Understandably, children tend to prefer the latter type!

The tradition of marking the days of Advent with some sort of calendar goes back to the beginning of the 1800s, but the period has been marked out as special in one way or another since the fourth century.

Why?

The Advent period has a triple-layered meaning in many churches. Sermons during the four weeks might refer to the time the Jewish people spent waiting for the Messiah or the time Christians spend in anticipation of the Second Coming. Overshadowing both of these is the simple, and very present, anticipation of the celebration of the birth of Christ. *Advent* or *adventus* is Latin for "coming" or "approaching."

Advent calendars help renew the excitement of the period every day, with children rushing each morning to see what picture or sweet treat is hidden behind the next door, until Christmas Day arrives.

2
Advent Wreaths

Who?

The practice of making midwinter wreaths was popular in northern Europe in the centuries before Christianity arrived. The Romans, famously, made wreaths of laurel leaves for their champions and leaders. Other people groups made evergreen wreaths.

But it took some creative thinking by German pastor Johann Hinrich Wichern to associate the wreath with the Advent period and develop its Christian symbolism.

Pastor Wichern devoted his life to "home missions," traveling all across Germany to establish Sunday schools, children's homes, and rescue stations for the destitute. He eventually became an inspector of prisons. Pastor Wichern was a Protestant, but before long both Protestant and the Catholic communities had enthusiastically embraced his new idea.

What?

The wreath was traditionally made of evergreen branches woven tightly into a circle. It would be laid horizontally (rather than vertically, as is the tradition in many American homes these days) and decorated with seeds, nuts, and pinecones. Being made virtually fireproof by nature, it made a convenient and attractive setting for candles.

These days many families hang decorated wreaths on their front doors to show they are celebrating Christmas. The horizontal version can still be found in churches, where a candle will be lit for each week of the Advent period. A fifth candle, usually in the middle of the wreath, is often used to represent Christ.

Where?

Originally the candles on the midwinter wreaths made by pagan peoples would have been offerings to tempt the "dying" sun to come back in springtime. They may have had some Christian associations in the Middle Ages.

Pastor Wichern, who founded a mission school in Munich, is said to have been constantly pestered by the children who wanted to know how long it was until Christmas. So, he set a cart wheel on its side, decorated it with leaves and branches, and placed a candle on each spoke with one in the center. The children got to light a candle each day and so could see Christmas Day, and the last candle, coming ever closer.

When?

Midwinter wreaths have been made since time immemorial. Pastor Wichern made his cart wheel "wreath" in 1839. The two traditions must have seemed ripe for combining, but the smaller versions were definitely preferable. After all, most people could weave some branches together, but not everyone had a cart wheel to spare or a place to display one. Churches made the wreaths and candles part of their annual services, and people took their own versions into their homes.

Perhaps surprisingly for such a firmly established Christmas tradition, the practice of hanging Advent wreaths on the doors of homes or lighting Advent candles in church did not reach the United States until the 1930s.

Why?

Pastor Wichern may have invented his Advent wreath to quiet down some excited children, as the legend suggests, but he probably also had the spiritual education of his wards at heart.

Christians who adopted the pagan wreaths probably had no difficulty equating the idea of never-ending life with the Eternal God. The practice of encouraging the sun to come back in the springtime fit well with the idea of waiting, excitedly, for the second coming of the Son of God.

Different churches attach different symbolisms to the four external candles, but they all encourage excited anticipation in the weeks before the Christ candle is lit.

3
Angels

Who?

The Bible doesn't say that Gabriel was the angel who announced the birth of Jesus to the shepherds, but it would seem very likely. After all it was he who told Mary she would give birth to the Son of God. The book of Luke tells of "an angel" making the announcement, but earlier in the story Gabriel described himself as the one who stands "in the presence of God; and am sent to speak unto thee" (Luke 1:19).

His name means "God is my strength," and he serves as God's messenger throughout the Bible. For an announcement of such magnificence, it seems highly unlikely God would have sent anyone else.

What?

Angels hold a position in creation somewhere between humanity and the divine. As such they are often used to carry important messages to humans or carry out God's will on earth. The name *angel* ultimately derives from the Greek word for "messenger."

The angels in the Bible seem to have presented themselves as men (sometimes as comforting messengers, sometimes as destroyers), but their beauty often leads to them being depicted in art as female. Most of the angels who adorn Christmas trees these days will be in the form of beautiful, adoring women with wings and halos. Surprisingly, no mention is made of angels having wings until the book of Revelation.

Where?

Gabriel and the other angels came directly from God and appeared, well, wherever there was a message that needed delivering! In the book of Luke the "heavenly host" appeared to the shepherds in a field in the night. Perhaps the shepherds were the only ones awake at that hour!

The Bible has them appearing in Israel and Judah, but there are very few countries where angelic appearances have not been recorded.

In family Christmases the angel (it will usually be either an angel or a star) takes pride of place at the very top of the tree, perhaps representing the idea that angels look down on us mortals from above.

When?

In the book of Genesis, an angel is sent to guard

the Garden of Eden. Angels play a major role in the book of Revelation. These two books cover the whole span of creation. So angels have always been with us and always will be.

But when should you put your angel on top of your Christmas tree? Some folk favor the tradition of twelve days before Christmas and for twelve days after. Increasingly, though, people put their tree (and their angel) up straight after Thanksgiving, thus making the most of the time available either to shop or to anticipate the birth of the Lord.

Why?

All through the Bible, angels carry messages, comfort the needy, and punish the unrepentant, but no errand from God could have been as important as the one trusted to the unnamed angel on the night of the first Christmas. He had to announce nothing less than the arrival of God on earth in the form of a newborn child!

He appeared in the middle of the night more than two millennia ago to tell some shepherds the good news, showing that God loved the humble. He was joined by "the heavenly host," who sang praises to God and promptly returned to heaven.

Why? For the salvation of all mankind. That's why!

4
Boxing Day

Who?

Rather wonderfully, the day after the one dedicated to Jesus Christ's birth is dedicated to Saint Stephen, Christianity's first-known martyr. In many countries Boxing Day is better known as St. Stephen's Day.

St. Stephen's Day, described as "the Feast of Stephen," is featured in the carol "Good King Wenceslas."

What?

Many countries where Christmas is a recognized holiday have some version of Boxing Day. It may be an officially sanctioned holiday from work, a day of spiritual observance, or simply a day of recovering from the excesses of Christmas.

In times when real holidays were much scarcer, Boxing Day undoubtedly had greater significance, but these days it does tend to get absorbed into the Christmas celebrations. Often it is little more than a chance to enjoy some major sporting events or simply catch up with the family and friends not seen on Christmas Day. (Not that those are unimportant things!)

Increasingly January sales are beginning on Boxing Day.

Where?

Boxing Day is recognized and celebrated in the United Kingdom and Commonwealth countries (countries associated with the former British Empire) across the world. Places with a strong Catholic or Lutheran tradition have also tended to preserve the idea of St. Stephen's Day. The combination of the two traditions means that one or the other is celebrated in many countries. However, many people in the United States have only read about the day.

For many the tradition will be celebrated in the home, but if we were to combine the charitable aspect of the day with the love displayed at Christmas, we could take a little Boxing Day generosity to some place where there was a need to be met.

When?

Boxing Day is celebrated on December 26. The Feast Day of St. Stephen, on which the tradition of Boxing Day stands, was proclaimed in 1083. Originally a day of remembrance and veneration, it became a day of charity to the poor and a valued holiday to people who worked in domestic service. It would have been one of the few days servants who lived in the grand homes of their masters were allowed time off to visit their families.

It was "on the Feast of Stephen" that Good King Wenceslas ventured out through the snow "deep and crisp and even" to take food and firewood to some poor neighbors.

Why?

Some believe the day got its name because the nobility and churches would traditionally empty their charity boxes to the poor on this day. Since medieval times, collecting boxes were left outside churches to collect money to feed the poor on St. Stephen's Day.

Another possible meaning of the term *Boxing Day* derives from the gifts the nobility gave their servants. Primarily concerned with making sure their grand celebrations went well, members of the nobility would have required their staff to work on Christmas Day and given them the next day off. The servants were presented with boxes to take home to their families. Leftover food would be a substantial part of these gifts.

But because the name of the day isn't easily explainable, an attempt was made in modern times to suggest that Boxing Day was the day children put their Christmas presents back in their boxes. The people who suggested it must never have had children!

5
Candy Canes

Who?

Legend has it that the choirmaster of Cologne Cathedral was the one who first bent straight white candy canes into their familiar inverted "J" shape. It wasn't to represent the name Jesus, as is often thought, but to represent the crooks of the shepherds to whom the angel announced the first Nativity.

August Imgard, a German immigrant, brought the tradition to Ohio. He is generally credited with being the first person in America to decorate a Christmas tree with candy canes.

Gregory Keller, a Catholic priest and brother-in-law of Bob McCormack, invented the first candy cane machine. Bob McCormack's company, Bob's Candies, then became *the* major candy cane manufacturer.

What?

Shaped sugar treats were probably the earliest form of candy and would have been made (when the ingredients were available) by hand in the home. The recipe includes sugar, corn syrup, cream of tartar, flavoring, and coloring. The hardening mixture could be pulled into shapes, but the most common shape would have been the straight cane.

The colored stripe and flavor were added much later in the candy cane's history.

The curve at the top of the cane (making it look like a shepherd's crook) was not intended to make it easy to hang on people's Christmas trees— but some combinations just work too well to be ignored!

Where?

Being made as treats for children, candy canes could have been around a long time and been made in many places without making it into recorded history. But where they come to the world's attention is in Cologne, Germany.

Like so many other European traditions, this one traveled with immigrants to the United States, where it was adopted and quickly became established as a Christmas tradition.

Bob's Candies, based in Georgia, was the first company to mass-produce candy canes.

Perhaps surprisingly, candy canes are much more popular in the United States than in Europe, where the tradition began.

When?

Candy treats might easily have been a part of pagan Yule festivals in northern Europe before Christianity arrived. The tradition persisted, and in 1670 we have the first recorded instance of their being used as a Christian symbol.

In 1847 August Imgard cut a spruce tree from the woods near his home in Wooster, Ohio, and decorated it with a tin star, paper decorations, and lots of candy canes. This is generally considered to be the first time a Christmas tree was *ever* decorated with candy canes in the United States.

Sometime in the 1950s Gregory Keller invented the candy cane machine and made mass production possible.

Why?

Why? Who needs an excuse for a sweet treat? Mothers would have made them to keep their children happy, and perhaps the Cologne choirmaster wanted to keep his choir quiet during a long Nativity (when they weren't supposed to be singing, of course!).

The familiar cane shape may have been meant to symbolize the shepherd's crook, or it may have symbolized the Great Shepherd, Jesus Christ Himself.

The red strip, so common in candy canes, is

said to represent Christ's blood, and the white color of the cane symbolizes His purity. Even the flavorings have meanings, with peppermint said to represent hyssop, the reed on which the crucified Jesus was offered a sponge to drink from.

6
Christingle

Who?

The man who is credited with conducting the very first Christingle service was Bishop Johannes de Watteville.

But the story that may have inspired the bishop tells of a group of poor children who wanted to present an offering at a Christmas service. Not being able to compete with the other rich offerings at the altar, they gave the most precious thing they had—an orange! Thinking it lacked something, each child added a decoration: a candle, a ribbon, and some little treats.

When the other children sneered at their efforts, the priest held it up as an offering of the very best kind, a gift from the heart!

What?

Christingle is a church tradition aimed specifically at children. It began as a way of trying to explain the significance of Christmas to little ones.

The Christingle itself is usually an orange or an

apple with a candle inserted at the top. A ribbon is tied around it, and four toothpicks are stuck into the orange through the ribbon. The toothpicks are decorated with little offerings of candy or fruit. The bottom half of the orange often is wrapped in aluminum foil.

More ornate metal globes are sometimes used as Christingles, but the simplicity and the humble nature of the usual ingredients are part of the charm of the tradition.

Where?

The Christingle service is believed to have originated in the Moravian Church, which originated in the lands that became known as Czechoslovakia (now the Czech Republic).

A Moravian bishop preaching to noble families in Marienborn Castle in Germany encouraged the children to show their understanding of Christmas in front of their parents and supplied them with the necessary accoutrements. That initial charming performance soon became a tradition.

The Children's Society, a charity caring for children in need, took the Christingle to England, but by then the Moravian Church had already taken it to Pennsylvania, in the United States. The two churches have since taken the tradition to many other countries across the world.

When?

The first Christingle service was held in 1747, but there were no oranges or apples (the other fruit sometimes used) involved. Each child held a candle wrapped in a red ribbon.

In 1756 the practice reached the New World, with the first American Christingle service being held in Bethlehem, Pennsylvania.

In 1968 it was introduced to the Anglican Church as a part of their Christmas celebrations.

There is no fixed date in the calendar for the Christingle service. When the service takes place is usually left up to the individual churches. It may be held any time between Advent and Epiphany, but it is often held on Christmas Eve.

Why?

The name *Christingle* means "Christ's light." It is significant that the ceremony is aimed at children, as Jesus asked us to come to Him like little children. It is a very effective way of reminding the little ones of the spiritual truth behind the decorations and the gifts.

The orange represents the world. The candle is the light of the world, or Jesus. The red ribbon reminds us that blood was spilled for our salvation. The fruits and candies represent God's blessings, and the four toothpicks symbolize either the four seasons, reminding us that God is with us all year round, or the four quarters of the world, reminding us that He is everywhere.

7
Christmas Carols

Who?

Francis of Assisi, that joyful man of God, is said to have been responsible for popularizing the idea of Christmas carols. Before his time there would have been chants or hymns sung in churches and abbeys. They would often have been complex arrangements that were never sung outside of church. Saint Francis is said to have taken them beyond cloister walls and made them easier for ordinary people to sing.

John Audelay, an English priest, wrote (or compiled) the first collection of "caroles of Cristemas."

Martin Luther and the Protestant Reformation embraced the singing of carols, with Luther personally authoring several.

Oliver Cromwell banned the singing of Christmas carols. It didn't last!

What?

What defines a carol? It is generally considered to be a song with religious content set to a joyful tune and arranged in a way that is easy for a crowd to sing. Of course, you wouldn't have to look far to find Christmas carols with no religious content or even a joyful tune. Popular usage at that time of year tends to determine what qualifies as a carol.

In the Middle Ages a carol was a circular dance during which the dancers also sang; so we have the group aspect, the joyful aspect, and, depending on the time of year, the songs may well have had religious significance.

Where?

The first songs with a specifically Christmas theme were written in Latin and sung in Rome. As the church spread across Europe, Christmas songs went with it. The twelfth-century French monk Adam of Saint Victor was the first to take religious lyrics and put them together with popular contemporary tunes, an important step on the journey from "Christmas song" to "Christmas carol." But his songs were in Latin, not French.

English hymnists, like nineteenth-century minister and poorhouse warden John Mason Neale, translated many Latin and French carols into English, paving the way for their eventual arrival in the New World. Not restricted by European traditions, American writers have added considerably to the canon of Christmas carols.

When?

The church in Rome sang Christmas songs as far back as the fourth century AD. One of those, "Of the Father's Love Begotten," was written by a poet who died around 413 AD and is still being sung to this day.

In the thirteenth century a tradition of carols being sung in "local" languages flourished. Carols, either written in English or translated into that language, first appeared in England in 1426.

In 1833 the English lawyer William Sandys brought together his compilation *Christmas Carols Ancient and Modern.*

The song believed to be the first American Christmas carol is "Jesus Is Born," written by Reverend John de Brébeuf.

Why?

If there is an emotion more appropriate to Christmas than any other, it must surely be joy. And can there be a better way to express joy than through song? Saint Francis of Assisi thought so when he made carols part of church services and encouraged their translation into the languages of the ordinary people.

For many people carols will simply be happy, catchy tunes to share in a party atmosphere. For others all that applies, but there will be a deeper meaning summed up in Psalm 30:4, which says, "Sing unto the LORD, O ye saints of his, and give thanks at the remembrance of his holiness."

8
Christmas Cookies

Who?
Mothers! For as long as mothers have been baking, they have been coming up with sweet little somethings for special occasions. (Of course, chefs and cooks of both sexes have taken up the tradition.)

Amazingly, the Crusaders of the Middle Ages played a part in the development of the cookie. Returning to Europe after fighting in the Holy Land, they brought with them a variety of exotic ingredients that made their way into Christmas cookies and into children's bellies.

The enthusiasm of the aforementioned children will have played a considerable part in keeping the tradition going!

Christmas cookies are now a major industry as well as a homemade treat.

What?
The word *cookie* comes from the Dutch word

koekje, meaning "little cake," and cookies come in a wonderful variety of tastes and shapes.

American Cookery by Amelia Simmons, published in 1796, gave the ingredients for cookies, then advised, "Kneed all together well, roll three quarters of an inch thick, and cut or stamp into shape and slice you please, bake slowly fifteen or twenty minutes; tho' hard and dry at first, if put in an earthen pot, and dry cellar, or damp room, they will be finer, softer and better when six months old."

The question has to be asked, would the children ever be prepared to wait that long?

Where?

Many nationalities have their own specialty cookie. The Norwegian Christmas cookie is called *Krumkake*. A waffle-type cookie, it is baked on a hot iron, then formed into a conical shape.

Sweden has *Pepparkakor*, thin gingersnap-style cookies that can be cut into any shape.

Pepernoten were originally baked in Holland, specifically for Saint Nicholas, on the fifth of December. Small, ball-shaped treats, they often contain aniseed and cinnamon.

Mexico has the *Reposteria*, which is a shortbread-style cookie coated in sugar and cinnamon.

Springerle are aniseed-flavored cookies from Germany and Austria.

Pennsylvania even has an official state cookie. It adopted the sugar cookie, brought to the United States by German immigrants, in 2001.

When?

Their size, durability and the fact that they are small enough to put into a travel bag mean that cookies have been a part of baking for as long as baking has existed. The inclusion of sugar in cookies first occurred in ancient Persia and spread from there across Europe.

By the fourteenth century cookies could be found at all levels of European society.

The introduction of cookie cutters to the United States from Germany at the end of the nineteenth century opened the way for cookies shaped like Christmas trees, candy canes, holly leaves, and so on.

The tradition of leaving cookies and milk out for Santa only became popular in the 1930s.

Why?

While gingerbread and other types of cookies have almost always been popular in Europe, their inclusion in Queen Victoria's Christmas Day meals caused some of them to make the transition from ordinary baked treats to full-blown Christmas cookies.

The fact that the tradition of leaving them for Santa became popular during the Great Depression would suggest that cookies were the ideal way for children to show they enjoyed sharing treats, even if they might not be receiving any.

And, when all else has been said and done, do we really need a reason to enjoy beautiful, delicious cookies at Christmastime?

9
Christmas Eve

Who?
The shepherds who were told of the birth of Christ didn't have much time to anticipate the event, but the Magi, or Wise Men, traveled far in anticipation, and, approaching Bethlehem, there must have been a night when they thought, "Tomorrow is the day!" Though it's unlikely they got there on the day of Jesus's birth, could they still be said to be the very first people to observe Christmas Eve?

In modern times Christmas Eve is a time for parents to breathe a sigh of relief and for children to excitedly pretend to be fast asleep (while actually listening for the sound of reindeer hooves on the roof!).

On this day churchgoers usually attend a service for private or communal devotions.

What?
Strangely, the night before Christmas Day is often

more spiritual than the day itself. All the shopping has been done, all the arrangements made, and everything has been set in place for the next day. Once the shops close, there is a lull in the chaos of organization, a time when often only churches are open. With no other distractions, people find time to give God their full attention.

Different churches observe the evening in different ways; some have a watch-night service, some vespers. In many churches the only illumination will come from candles, helping to create a mood of prayer and contemplation.

Where?

The very first Christmas Eve happened in the same place every Christmas Eve has happened since. Just outside Bethlehem—and all around the world! The only difference is on that first evening very few were aware of the importance of the event; now people celebrate it all around the world.

On Christmas Eve, 1968, the tradition moved beyond this world when astronauts Frank Borman, Jim Lovell, and Bill Anders read an extract from the Book of Genesis from on board the spaceship Apollo 8. The twentieth century's equivalent of the three Wise Men did indeed "traverse afar." They broadcast their message to the world from the moon's orbit!

When?

Although the name implies an event that takes place in the evening, the term *Christmas Eve* generally applies to the whole of December 24. It ends at midnight.

So when was the first Christmas Eve? No one knows for sure. Dates for the birth of Jesus range from 3 BC to 29 AD. The reference to the shepherds still being on the hills with their sheep makes it seem unlikely the first Christmas Eve took place in midwinter.

What does it matter? As a time of anticipation of the arrival of Jesus, December 24 simply serves as a reminder that the whole year round—every year—might be spent in similar anticipation.

Why?

For many children, getting to sleep will be nearly impossible on Christmas Eve, so excited will they be about the gifts they hope to get in the morning! Hints may have been given as to the nature of those brightly wrapped boxes and clues offered just to tease. Then, of course, there is the opening of those presents!

The world waited a long time for Jesus to arrive. We were given all too brief a visit. And now it waits for him to return.

Christmas Eve is a reminder of those times

of waiting, waiting for the gift we already know so much about but that will surely outstrip all expectations.

10
Christmas Lights

Who?

Before the coming of electricity, church services would only have been illuminated by daylight or candlelight. Some churches even resisted installing their own candelabras, asking families to bring their own candles or lamps, as *they* were the true lights of the church!

A woodcut picture of Queen Victoria's candle-lit Christmas tree helped bring the tradition of tree lights to the United States.

Sir Joseph Swan decorated actors playing angels in an operetta with electric lighting, inspiring the term "fairy lights."

President Grover Cleveland switched on the first electrically lit Christmas tree at the White House.

Now electric Christmas lights appear in most homes and many public spaces as part of the celebrations.

What?

It's no coincidence that so many of our Christmas lights look like candles. That's exactly what they would have been once upon a time, real candles sitting on the branches of real trees! But, of course, as the tradition moved indoors, that became a dangerous option.

Now tiny electrical lights can be produced in strings, nets, and even made into sculpture shapes. They can shine steadily, flash intermittently, or even switch on and off in time to music.

The reduction in price caused by mass production (way down from the $300 cost to light a tree in the early 1900s) has led to "fairy lights" being used for all kinds of events.

Where?

The idea of lighting up a tree with candles came from Germany and moved to England with the German-born relatives (and husband) of Queen Victoria.

American Thomas Edison's work with electric light was directly responsible for the invention of Christmas lights. The vice president of his company produced Christmas lights only two years after Edison patented the electric lightbulb.

Now shopping malls and sporting arenas cover themselves in light displays to encourage people to join in the festive fun.

Many homeowners go to incredible lengths to illuminate their homes at Christmas, sometimes just for fun but often as a way of raising money for charity.

When?

Originally candles were stuck to the Christmas tree branches with melted wax. It took until almost the end of the nineteenth century for candleholders to come into fashion.

The vice president of the Edison Electric Light Company, Edward Johnson, had eighty red, white, and blue miniature lightbulbs made for his Christmas tree in 1882. This is believed to have been the first time electric lights decorated a Christmas tree. Unfortunately the cost was prohibitive, and it wasn't until almost fifty years later that affordable Christmas lights arrived in the shops.

In 1895 the White House displayed its first electrically lit Christmas tree, encouraging the fashion to spread across America.

Why?

There are lots of reasons for liking Christmas lights! We could be representing the Christmas star or the lamps in the stable where Christ lay. We may be harking back to seemingly simpler and cozier times, when people gathered around the lamp and held services by candlelight. In the early days of electricity it would most certainly have been a status symbol. It might just be because they are pretty, and people like pretty things.

Or it might be that those bright, sparkly lights remind us there is something purer, something brighter in each of us than what we show the world through the rest of the year.

11
Christmas Markets

Who?

The German, Austrian, and Polish peoples came up with the idea of midwinter or Christmas markets. It is an idea that does seem better suited to dark, cold nights (although the markets are open through the day and well into the evening.)

Faith-based groups often set up Nativity scenes, and some even welcome the Christ child in when the market begins. But mostly it is a good opportunity for small traders and craftspeople to make the most of a Christmas shopping spree that might otherwise pass them by.

While most markets cater to local people, some have grown large enough to become tourist attractions in their own right.

What?

The Christmas market may be simply a gathering of local traders selling their wares. But they can often be much larger, incorporating amusement parks, ice rinks, and live music. Many markets have become so organized that instead of makeshift stalls they have what amounts to miniature Alpine cabins to sell from.

The goods for sale will be anything festive! Hot food and warm drinks will feature heavily, as will warm clothing and Christmas decorations.

If you have ever joined Nat King Cole in singing about "chestnuts roasting on an open fire" and wondered what they tasted like, the Christmas market would be a good place to find out.

Where?
The Christmas market idea seems to have developed in Germany and surrounding countries. It has spread across Europe and is now a major feature in the festive celebrations of a handful of American cities.

Dresden in Germany, Vienna in Austria, and Bautzen in Poland can each make a claim to having the oldest Christmas Market.

The markets are usually held in town squares or city centers, public places that are close to traffic and allow pedestrians to wander and shop but are large enough to have, on some occasions, several hundred market stalls.

The Christmas market in Edinburgh, Scotland, actually boardwalks over part of an ancient cemetery.

When?

A "December market" was held in Vienna as far back as 1294. At some point this became known as a Christmas market. Other markets sprang up around the same time. The Christmas market in Strasbourg, France, has been held continually in the same location around the cathedral (wars permitting) since 1570.

Traditionally, the markets tend to open on the first week of Advent, or simply the first day of December. Being primarily sales opportunities, they try to make the most of the festive season, stopping on the most suitable day before Christmas (often Christmas Eve!). Of course, they are very good fun as well!

Why?

Another name for the Christmas market is the *Christkindlmarkt*, or "Christ-child market," which might imply a spiritual origin. But while the traders and chambers of commerce who instigated them may well have been spiritual men, the market (in the days before High Street stores) would simply have been a good retail opportunity and a way to liven up the dreary midwinter.

Strangely, though, they often do have a feeling of camaraderie, a way of bringing people together. Usually everyone is cold, happy, and sharing in an experience that only happens once a year. Materialistic or not, the Christmas market is a good place to find some free Christmas spirit!

12

Christmas Pudding/Mince Pies

Who?

The traditional round shape and general recipe for the Christmas pudding was established in Victorian England. Before that it was made, in various forms, by agricultural folk all across Europe.

The Victorians added some of the more exotic spices and ingredients, making it a dish for the wealthier members of society. Thankfully those ingredients are now more easily available, and whether or not a Christmas pudding appears on a Christmas dinner table is more related to the individual tastes of the family involved than money and social status.

Jesus and the twelve apostles are represented in the mix, which is traditionally supposed to have thirteen ingredients.

What?

Christmas pudding is the traditional second course

to the Christmas dinner (third, if there is a starter). It consists of flour, suet, bread crumbs, spices, nutmeg, cinnamon, brown sugar, sultanas, raisins, currants, mixed peel, almonds, apple, orange, lemon, eggs, rum, barley wine, and so on. There is no definite recipe because different families have different ways of preparing their family's favorite Christmas pudding. Some families have recipes handed down over several generations.

Amazingly Christmas puddings and mince pies began as the same thing. Meat would be preserved during the winter months by wrapping it in what was basically Christmas pudding mix, becoming, in essence, large meat pies. In modern times, though, meat has generally disappeared from Christmas puddings and pies.

Where?

The mix that became Christmas pudding and mince pies was commonly used among farming folk in Europe. It was particularly popular in Germany, and the prince-elector of Hanover brought it to Great Britain when he became King George the First. He was affectionately known in Britain as "the Pudding King."

The habit of hanging the pudding in a cloth for several weeks to allow it to "ripen," thus giving it its distinctive spherical shape, was firmly established in Victorian England. Since coming to the United States and becoming more commercially available, the pudding has developed a much more practical flat base—to stop it rolling off the plate!

When?

The original mix that became the Christmas pudding and the mince pie is known to have been used as a meat preservative as far back as the early fifteenth century.

In medieval times the church ruled that Christmas puddings should be made on the twenty-fifth Sunday after Trinity Sunday (Trinity Sunday being late May or early June, depending on the church and the year).

The mix was known by many different names, such as "pottage," "plum porridge," and "plum pudding." The first time it is known to have been referred to as Christmas pudding was in the cookbook *Modern Cookery for Private Families*, published in 1845.

Why?

So if the Christmas pudding mix was used to preserve meat, the mince pies that evolved from it must have been quite substantial. Why then, do we now have mince pies that are so small?

It's all down to Oliver Cromwell banning

Christmas! The original mince pies were large enough to feed whole families, but difficult to hide. People celebrating Christmas in Cromwell's England risked jail if they were caught, so they had to be prepared to hide all signs of Christmas from Cromwellian spies.

So the pies became "bite-sized," and, more often than not, Cromwell's men were left with nothing more than a delicious aroma—and no proof!

13
Christmas Stockings

Who?

The man behind the unlikely tradition of Christmas stockings is usually thought to have been Nikolaos of Myra. He was a Greek Christian who became bishop of Myra, a city of Asia Minor.

Nikolaos, or Saint Nicholas as he became known, was a kind man, and his faith was such that he became known as Nicholas the Wonder-worker for the miracles he performed. The title "Saint Nicholas" was expressed in Dutch as *Sinterklass*, and this came into American English as "Santa Claus."

Nicholas's personality and piousness was such that he is revered by both Catholic and Protestant churches. He is the patron saint of sailors, children, archers, students, and even thieves!

What?

Christmas stockings used to be the stockings people actually wore. They would be hung from the mantelpiece in anticipation of finding small gifts inside them on Christmas Day morning.

Some families fill stockings for their children with little "stocking fillers" and put the larger gifts under the Christmas tree. But in poorer times and places the stocking fillers might be all the child received. Cold ash from the fire was often used to fill out stockings with only a few gifts. Naughty children traditionally received a lump of coal.

In modern times large, decorated Christmas stockings can be bought in stores. And some of them even come already filled with treats!

Where?

The city of Myra, where Nicholas was bishop, was a part of Lycea during his lifetime. These days it is known as Demre and is situated on the Antalya coast in Turkey. Nicholas was a Greek Christian, and a sizable community of Greek Christians lived in the same location until the 1920s.

The original stockings would have been hung up at the fireplace to dry overnight. In modern times stockings might be pinned to the wall or hung by the foot of a child's bed.

Bishop Nicholas's kind gift has become part of children's Christmases wherever the holiday is celebrated—although some people do leave out shoes rather than stockings!

When?

Nikolaos of Myra was born in 270 AD and died in 343 AD, so the idea of leaving gifts in stockings probably originated in the early fourth century. It continues to be a Christmas favorite seventeen centuries later.

Those families who lay aside a "Christmas room" and decorate it all through December might hang their stockings up at any time during that month. Otherwise the Christmas stocking is usually hung up on Christmas Eve, although, with fewer houses having fireplaces these days, parents may have to be more imaginative about where they are hung.

The stocking is often the first thing explored on Christmas Day morning!

Why?

Bishop Nicholas (before he was a saint) was wandering through town one evening, according to legend, when he overheard a father's lament. His three daughters all had men they wanted to marry, but he couldn't provide them with dowries, so the weddings couldn't go ahead.

Nicholas waited until the middle of the night then slipped into the man's house. He carried with him three bags of gold, one for each daughter. Looking around for a place to put them, he spotted the daughters' stockings hanging over the fire to dry. He left the bags of gold in the stockings—and a Christmas tradition was born!

14
Christmas Trees

Who?

Saint Boniface was an eighth-century English missionary to the pagan tribes in the land that became Germany. Finding that they worshipped a large oak dedicated to Thor, Boniface decided to chop it down. If Thor were the true God, he told the assembled tribesmen, then Boniface would die. If he didn't, it was proof that his God was the mightier one.

After one stroke of the ax, a strong wind came and blew the oak over. No one was going to argue with Boniface after that!

Legend has it that he planted a fir tree in place of the oak, and this became the first Christmas tree.

What?

Trees, decorated and worshipped in the woods, were eventually replaced by smaller, felled trees placed outside shops to advertise their business. Gradually, smaller trees made their way into homes.

Today we have the choice of natural trees or artificial ones that can be put away and reused year after year.

Around forty million real, or specially grown, trees are bought in the United States each year during the Christmas period.

An angel or a star is usually placed on top of the tree to symbolize one of the two ways the news of Christ's birth was proclaimed (by an angel to the shepherds or by a star to the Wise Men).

Where?

Trees first became a part of the Christmas celebrations in northern Germany. Some of those celebrations ended with the tree being set on fire!

Prussian troops took the tradition into southern Germany, but the Christmas tree stayed firmly rooted in that area for a considerable time. Germans traveling abroad might delight their friends with their decorated trees, but it wasn't until the time of Queen Victoria (who was related to the German royal family) that the tradition became popular in the United Kingdom. From the United Kingdom it spread to the United States, although people in many states claim (with good cause) that German ancestors brought the tradition directly to them!

When?

Saint Boniface chopped the Donar Oak (Thunder Oak) down in 723 AD. But the first recorded use of a Christmas tree took place in an Estonian monastery in 1441.

In 1781 German soldiers sent to defend Quebec against America during the Revolutionary War celebrated Christmas with a decorated tree.

In 1848 a picture of Queen Victoria standing by a decorated Christmas tree was circulated throughout the United States in *Godey's Magazine and Lady's Book*. (The picture was altered, removing Victoria's tiara to make it look less royal and more like one of an ordinary family.) From that time onward American families increasingly made the Christmas tree a part of their family celebrations.

Why?

Trees made convenient gathering points for pagan, midwinter celebrations. Offerings would be made and fires lit to encourage the rebirth of the sun and the fresh life it would bring. It made sense for the early Christians to adopt and adapt this into a celebration of the birth of the life-giving Son of God.

The first decorations placed on Christmas trees were wax candles, which may have indicated Jesus being "the Light of the World" or may simply have been a way of emulating chandeliers.

These days, though, the tree makes a wonderful gathering place and the perfect frame from which to hang candy canes, lights, and other sparkly stuff.

15
Christmas Gifts

Who?

The first Christmas gift was undoubtedly from God to us, and it was Jesus. The next ones were presented to Christ himself by the Magi (or the Wise Men, or the three kings).

Across the world, children wait excitedly for a variety of gift bringers, the most famous of whom is Santa Claus. In Scandinavia a gnome called *Julenisse* delivers the gifts; in Holland it is *Sinterklaas;* Russian children get their presents from Grandfather Frost; in Spain the three kings perform the honors; and in Italy *La Befana* brings gifts—but not until Twelfth Night!

In almost every country, though, hardworking parents are usually the gift-bearer's main helpers!

What?

The Magi famously presented the Christ child with frankincense, gold, and myrrh, representing His roles as a priest, a king, and a healer.

Since then we have given gifts as a symbol of

sharing in His love, but the gifts themselves have varied with location and availability. Sometimes they have been treats; at other times they might be necessities.

In modern times, however, Christmas gifts have become ever more electronic and expensive.

But the last word on gifts has to go to columnist and author Burton Hillis, who once wrote, "The best of all gifts around any Christmas tree: the presence of a happy family all wrapped up in each other."

Where?

Many Christmas cards still paint a picture of bulging stockings hanging from a mantelpiece over a roaring fire. Thankfully, from a safety point of view, this image is rarely translated into real life anymore.

Once upon a time a child might only have gotten the gifts that could be fitted into his or her sock (and in hard times that sock might have been bulked out by ashes), but modern children must be glad that isn't usually the case anymore.

In some places a room is laid aside, decorated, and filled with the children's presents. This room is kept locked, and the curtains closed, until Christmas morning.

When?

Giving gifts at Christmastime is such an essential part of it that it seems hard to imagine a time when it didn't happen. In medieval times gifts weren't given at Christmas at all; rather they might be given at Twelfth Night. Some countries, notably Spain, still maintain this tradition.

Some softer-hearted parents might allow their children to open one present before bedtime on Christmas Eve, but usually Christmas morning is when all the presents get opened. Of course, the children are at liberty to make Christmas morning come around as early as they possibly can—as many a bleary-eyed, but hopefully amused, parent has found out!

Why?

The image of the gifts of the Magi is so strongly associated with Christmas that the tradition of giving gifts probably originated with them. It may also have been a way for the pious to give thanks for the blessing God had bestowed on them. There may also have been an element of feeding the hungry and clothing the poor in His name.

These admirable sentiments still exist with some people who request that gifts be made in their name to charities. But for most of us these days the primary reason for giving gifts at Christmas is to see that look of delight on the faces of our loved ones.

16

Christmas Pageants

Who?

The original Christmas pageant took place when the shepherds, and later the Magi, came to visit the infant Christ. The characters were the real-life Mary, Joseph, Jesus, and any animals that happened to be in the stable.

Francis of Assisi started a "living Nativity," where people enacted the Holy Family and their visitors. The church adopted the idea, but in many instances replaced it with sculpted and molded tableaux.

These days the pageant's roles are most often played by excited children, while their parents paint scenes, create costumes, and help with lines. What was originally a family "performance" has become a family event once again.

What?

Christmas pageants are living depictions of the event that all of Christianity stems from—the birth of Jesus Christ. It can be serious and reverential, but, in keeping with the joy of the salvation it represents, it is usually a fun event, where children and adults recreate that humble stable and the events that took place in it.

Secular society isn't always welcoming of such overtly faith-filled displays, but thankfully there are still enough churches, community centers, schools, homes, towns, and cities willing to recreate the greatest story ever told for the Christmas pageant to be a favorite and much-anticipated part of the festive season.

Where?

The scene depicted in countless Christmas pageants took place in Bethlehem in Judea. Bethlehem is the city referred to in the song "Once in Royal David's City." It was the birthplace of King David.

Frances of Assisi's living Nativity took place in a cave near Greccio in Italy, perhaps inspired by some traditions that say the birth took place in a cave outside Bethlehem rather than in a stable.

Modern Christmas pageants might be held in community halls, churches, or schools. Larger sponsored events might be held in public areas. But those who believe will find a way and a place to celebrate the event, wherever they might be.

When?

No one knows for sure when the Nativity occurred, but common consent has it being in the first year AD. It may have been a few years before or several years after.

The live Nativity staged by Francis of Assisi took place in 1223. During the next century the tradition spread so that almost every church in Italy had one.

Modern pageants are held in December, but dates will depend on "earthly" factors such as venue availability. The most emotionally evocative date is, of course, Christmas Day, but, with most people spending that day with their families, the last opportunity for a pageant is often Christmas Eve.

Why?

Children learn through play, and they love play-acting. So pretending to be shepherds, Wise Men, Mary, and Joseph is surely the ideal way of learning about the miraculous events of so long ago.

Those who already know the story offer their pageants as a tribute of love and a way of keeping the story alive in people's memories. As well as providing an entertaining show, the organizers usually hope the occasion plants a seed of belief in the minds of some who have never considered faith before.

Why did those real-life characters enact the first-ever Christmas pageant? For nothing less than the salvation of all mankind!

17
Family Gatherings

Who?

When God came down to earth, He could have come in glory, riding clouds and flashing lightning. He could have walked into the most opulent palace in the world and declared it His. Who would have argued? Instead He appeared in a stable and entrusted Himself to—a family! Then that family had an odd assortment of visitors popping in. So, you see, right from the very first time, family gatherings have always been at the heart of Christmas.

When you think that God is our Father, we are His children, and He came to visit us, what could be more beautifully appropriate than family gatherings at Christmas?

What?

Family is what you make it. The Holy Family was not really all that conventional. Mary was probably in her teens; Joseph may have been a much older man. She carried a child that not only wasn't his but also was God's! And they both talked to angels!

By comparison even the most unusual of modern families seems quite ordinary. If you are lucky enough to have a "conventional" family, appreciate it, and spread the blessing. If you aren't, then remember, a family is where love is, and you can make one of your own by putting love where there was none.

Where?

That "First Family" of Christianity spent the first Christmas in Bethlehem, a town about eight miles from Jerusalem and with an illustrious history. Sometimes called Ephrata, Bethlehem is referred to frequently throughout the Old Testament.

But their gathering didn't take place in a nice, comfortable home, or even in an uncomfortable one—it happened in a stable! So it doesn't really matter if your family gathering takes place in a beautiful house with its own grounds or in a trailer or in a fast-food restaurant. Jesus has already proven that He doesn't mind about the location, just so long as you remember to invite Him along!

When?

Scholars aren't really sure when Joseph and Mary became "Mommy" and "Daddy." So, by common consensus, they agree on the first year AD, but it could have been a year or two earlier, or several years later.

These days the date is, thankfully, more certain, and people can plan in advance. Christmas, perhaps more than any other holiday, is the time families want to be together. Airports and railroads will be busier in the lead-up to December 25 than at any other time of the year.

How long they stay after that depends on how well the family gets on and how soon the Christmas spirit wears off!

Why?

As families, we are often more like groups of individuals, and that can cause friction, but Christmas is a reason to come together that is bigger than any one of us. The reason at the heart of it all is love, and no matter how badly or otherwise we get on with our families, deep down we all want to be loved by them. That longing may have been what brought God down to earth to be with His children.

Christmas is about God and family. If you can be with your family, then love them for His sake. If you can't, then gather some of His other children to you and love *them*.

18
Greetings Cards

Who?

The Chinese invented greetings cards. They (and much later the Egyptians) sent cards celebrating the New Year.

Homemade cards were probably being exchanged for different events, including Christmas, before Sir Henry Cole produced the first commercially available Christmas card. He designed the world's first stamp, invented a prize-winning teapot, and wrote children's books. As founder of the Victoria and Albert Museum, in London, he had the ear of the royal family and was often affectionately referred to as "Old King Cole" by the press.

The man who painted the template for the card was John Callcott Horsley, who painted some of the artwork currently decorating the British Houses of Parliament.

What?

The ancient Egyptians sent New Year greetings on papyrus scrolls. Fifteenth-century Germans made them from woodcuts. Before 1843 they would have been handwritten and hand delivered. Even after Sir Henry Cole's invention, many would keep on being handmade, his printed ones being quite expensive at a shilling apiece.

Mass production brought the price down and helped create a major industry.

The very first Christmas card showed a family celebrating but also depicted the feeding of the hungry and clothing of the poor, intentions the One whose birthday Christmas represents would surely have appreciated.

Printed on the front were the words, "A Merry Christmas and a Happy New Year to You."

Where?

The cards sent in ancient China and ancient Egypt were only for the ruling classes. The postal services that followed were highly localized and only for the wealthy.

In 1680 the Penny Post system was introduced in London, bringing the service within reach of ordinary people who wanted to send letters within ten miles of that city. In 1792 Benjamin Franklin set up the forerunner of the U.S. Postal Service.

The idea spread, and delivery costs came down to the point where even worldwide mail became affordable. Now people can send cards to friends and relatives in almost every corner of the world. And they do! Basically, wherever there is a postal system, someone will be sending greetings cards.

When?
Sir Henry Cole produced the first commercial Christmas cards in 1843.

He had taken part in the reform of the Penny Post, only three years before, so getting people to post cards at Christmas probably served his bank balance very well.

In 1875 German émigré Louis Prang brought the tradition of the printed card to America. Though he produced many different types of printed material, he is principally known today as "the father of the American Christmas card."

In the mid-1980s greeting cards of all kinds moved into the electronic age, and for the first time, people with Internet access were able to send "cards" to each other via e-mail.

Why?
In previous centuries the majority of the population lived and died in the same small area. Christmas cards and the postal system came along at a time

when industrialization, political activism, and better transport were changing all that. Perhaps more than any other time in human history, people were separated from family and friends by vast distances, and those distances probably never seemed greater than at Christmastime.

A Christmas card, despite only being thick, decorated paper, was an affordable way of conveying a lot of love across continents and over oceans. No wonder they are traditionally displayed prominently throughout the festive season and often saved for years!

19

It's a Wonderful Life

Who?

Philip Van Doren Stern, a writer, editor, and Civil War historian, wrote the story that *It's a Wonderful Life* was based on. Frank Capra bought the rights from RKO for the same amount they paid for it. RKO must have thought they were doing well by breaking even.

Director Frank Capra claims James Stewart was always his first choice for the role of George Bailey.

Donna Reed took the role of Mary Bailey, which Ginger Rogers had been offered but considered too bland.

Henry Travers, who played Clarence the angel, had been an architect in England before taking to the stage.

Lionel Barrymore was George Bailey's nemesis, Henry F. Potter.

What?

It's a Wonderful Life started off as a short story called "The Greatest Gift." Philip Van Doren Stern could not get a publisher for it, so he self-published a few copies. In less than a year the story caught the attention of the film industry.

The film version tells of George Bailey, a small-town boy who yearns for travel and adventure but, through one circumstance after another, is kept home in Bedford Falls, NY. Convinced his life has been a waste, he decides to end it all. But before he can do that, a trainee angel named Clarence turns up to show him what the world would have been like without him.

Where?

It's a Wonderful Life shows two sides of America. The fictional small town of Bedford Falls is a charming place; though not without its problems, it's a place where decent people do the right thing and kindness generally makes everything right.

Potterville is what Bedford Falls would have become if George Bailey had never lived. It is a neon-lit, noisy, harsh place, where people look out for number one and money rules.

Critics argued over which version of the town was the least realistic. But, in truth, both existed in America at the time and probably still do.

Potterville might be easier to find, but Bedford Falls is still out there!

When?

The idea for "The Greatest Gift" came to Philip Van Doren Stern in a dream in the late 1930s. He sent it to friends as a Christmas present in 1943. RKO bought the rights in 1944, and Capra bought it from them in 1945.

It's a Wonderful Life was due to be released in 1947 but was released in December 1946, which meant that it didn't go up against *Miracle on 34th Street* in the Oscars. The film was nominated for five Oscars but, amazingly, won none.

In 1990, *It's a Wonderful Life* was deemed culturally significant enough by the Library of Congress to be preserved in the National Film Registry.

Why?

Some stories just need to be told! Philip Van Doren Stern didn't claim to have created the story. It came to him in a dream. Frank Capra, who made the film, eventually said it didn't seem like something he had created but more like something with a life of its own. He once compared himself to a father whose son had gone on to become president. "It's the kid who did the work," he said, referring to his film as "the kid."

Perhaps, at a time when the world had just been to war, humanity needed reminding that, as Clarence the angel said, "Each man's life touches so many other lives."

20
"Jingle Bells"

Who?

James Lord Pierpont, son of a pastor and uncle of the banker J. P. Morgan, wrote "Jingle Bells." At age fourteen he ran away to sea, returning nine years later. Pierpont later moved across the country, leaving his wife and children with his parents, to take advantage of business opportunities caused by the California Gold Rush.

His business failed, and he returned home, eventually accepting a position as church organist in Savannah, Georgia, in the church where his brother was pastor. This position allowed the musical side of his personality to flourish.

Several of his compositions were performed professionally in his lifetime, and Bob Dylan based his song "Nettie Moore" on Pierpont's "Gentle Nettie Moore."

What?

"Jingle Bells," or "One Horse Open Sleigh," as it

was originally called, is one of the most recognizable of all Christmas carols. It has no religious content, but its joyful imagery and catchy chorus make it a favorite with all ages.

Jingle bells aren't actually a particular type of bell. The phrase is an encouragement to jingle the bells on the horses' harnesses with some exuberant sleigh driving.

The song tells of a young man collecting a young woman in his sleigh, but he drives too fast and tips them both out of it. Undeterred, he decides to keep the fun going by doing it all over again another night.

Where?

"One Horse Open Sleigh" was written not in a sleigh nor in a tavern, as popular legends have it. Pierpont was friendly with the owner of a boardinghouse and visited there to play the piano. Hearing him try out a new tune, the boardinghouse owner, Mrs. Waterman, praised his composition and encouraged him to put words to it. Mrs. Waterman's boardinghouse later became a tavern, giving rise to the idea that Pierpont, the son of a minister, wrote songs in a drinking den.

The boardinghouse was in Medford, Massachusetts. The town is rightly proud of the connection and commemorates it with a plaque.

When?

According to the commemoration plaque in Medford, "One Horse Open Sleigh" was written in 1850, around the time Pierpont would have been considering his move to California. It wasn't published until seven years later while Pierpont was giving music lessons and playing the organ at his brother's church. Two years later the piece was rereleased with the new title "Jingle Bells or the One Horse Open Sleigh."

Just before Christmas in 1965 the astronauts aboard Gemini 6 reported seeing a fast-moving object, driven by a man in red. Then they gave Mission Control a rendition of "Jingle Bells"!

Why?

Despite being a Christmas favorite, "Jingle Bells" was actually a Thanksgiving song. The only connection with Christmas is the idea of riding in a sleigh. Of course, Santa rides a sleigh, but his is pulled by reindeer, not horses.

Historians in Medford, Massachusetts, suggest Pierpont was inspired by Thanksgiving sleigh races held every year in the town. Young men driving "cutters," or single-horse sleighs, would race through the snow from Medford town square to the center of nearby Malden. It was an exciting event, and the drivers would have been popular among the young women of both towns. Pierpont's composition wonderfully describes the thrill and joy of it all.

21
"Joy to the World"

Who?

While he didn't compose "Joy to the World," the man who inspired it may actually have been King David! And Isaac Watts based his song on Psalm 98.

Watts, who wrote around 750 hymns, is often referred to as the father of English hymnody.

The music was composed by Lowell Mason, who also came up with the tune to "Mary Had a Little Lamb." Mason composed over sixteen hundred hymn tunes.

"Joy to the World" has been recorded by many choirs and artists over the years, including Andy Williams, the Supremes, Mariah Carey, and Whitney Houston.

What?

Isaac Watts, a theologian and writer, lived in a time when songs sung in church were nearly always based on the psalms or other Bible verses. His song "Joy to the World" was part of a collection of songs based on biblical writings. It was titled *The Psalms of David: Imitated in the Language of the New Testament and Applied to the Christian State and Worship.*

Lowell Mason's music "Antioch" is believed to have been based on a piece by classical composer George Frideric Handel.

At the end of the twentieth century, "Joy to the World" held the record for being the most-published Christmas hymn in the United States.

Where?

Isaac Watts was friendly with Sir Thomas Abney and his wife, Lady Mary. Their manor house in Stoke Newington, in England, had extensive gardens, which Watts used to enjoy.

After Sir Thomas's death, Watts moved into Abney House. He lived there with Sir Thomas's widow and daughter until his death later that year. But there had been many years for sitting in the grounds of Abney House, wandering by the river, watching wildlife, and writing. The Abney House gardens were the place of inspiration for many of his works, including "Joy to the World."

Lowell Mason did his composing in Boston, where he was a banker and a choirmaster.

When?

The Psalms of David: Imitated in the Language of the New Testament and Applied to the Christian State and Worship, including "Joy to the World," was published in 1719.

Lowell Mason took the original tune and adapted it, borrowing heavily from Handel, into the tune we are familiar with 120 years later.

At the age of forty-five, Watts's ill health led him to cut back on his preaching duties. Not wishing that his increased free time should be wasted, he set himself the daunting task of setting the psalms to verse. "Joy to the World" was probably written during this period.

Why?

Despite being one of the world's most popular Christmas hymns, "Joy to the World" is not, in fact, about Christmas or the birth of Christ. The "joy" that Isaac Watts had in mind was to be when Jesus *returned* to the world—in other words, the Second Coming!

Watts, the son of a nonconformist English preacher, went on to become a nonconformist preacher himself. The return of his Savior to this world would surely have been the greatest joy he could have conceived.

Watts's prolific writing output probably

stemmed from a childhood habit of rhyming nearly continually. When he was once punished for it, he apologized—in rhyme.

22

"Merry Christmas"

Who?

Despite its being a Christian tradition, people of faith, no faith, and other faiths all recognize wishing others a Merry Christmas as an established fact. And while some may object to being wished a Merry Christmas because it is seen as not being of their tradition, most people recognize and share in the warmth and good feeling that is conveyed in the greeting. Friends can share it with a hug, children with an excited squeal, and strangers with a handshake or a happy wave.

We might add "and a Happy New Year" to the end of the greeting, but only Santa Claus is allowed to add the "Ho, ho, ho!" at the beginning!

What?

In the festive season you might be wished a Merry Christmas or a Happy Christmas. Why the difference?

Well, *merry* was an Old English word for "pleasant." But this changed during the reign of Queen Victoria. Strong drink was playing a disruptive role in the newly industrialized society. People who were drunk enough to be troublesome were referred to as being "merry."

Queen Victoria disliked sending Christmas greetings tainted with such a disreputable image. She started sending "Happy Christmas" cards, and others followed her example.

Another explanation suggests that the greeting is a mispronunciation of "Mary Christmas," encouraging us to celebrate the event as Mary did—by presenting Jesus to the world.

Where?

As with so many old traditions, we can trace this one back to "Merry Olde England."

These days we think of the word *merry* as meaning joyful, just a bit above ordinary happiness, but back then it was spelled *mirige* or *myrige* and simply meant "pleasant." Hence Merry Olde England was a time when the summers were warm, the fields were producing plenty of food, taxes were low, and there were no more than the normal number of wars going on. Life was good!

Now the tradition and the greeting are known around the world—and are especially valued in lands where conditions aren't so merry.

When?

When did people first start wishing each other a Merry Christmas? The answer to that is lost in time, but we do know that the carol "We Wish You a Merry Christmas" was being sung in the fifteen hundreds. For it to have been given a tune and written down, the greeting itself must have been firmly established and so is probably very much older.

Different versions of *Merry Christmas* in different languages have probably been exchanged for as long as Christmas has been celebrated.

There is no set time to begin wishing people a Merry Christmas, but usually sometime in the second half of December is acceptable.

Why?

There are lots of special or holy days in the calendar. Very few of them have a greeting of their own. But isn't it fitting that a day of such significance should have a form of words that can be exchanged by friends and strangers alike? After all, the first Christmas was for all mankind!

Given the variety of holidays and festivals now taking their place in the "holiday season," wishing someone a Merry Christmas might be a statement of Christian faith, but its usage is wider than that these days and is often simply a way of wishing someone a pleasant and peaceful time at Christmas.

23

Miracle on 34th Street

Who?

Edmund Gwenn was an English actor, born in 1877. His career, spanning over eighty films and innumerable stage plays, was interrupted by both world wars. Two years after World War II he won an Oscar for his portrayal of Kris Kringle.

Maureen O'Hara was already a successful actress, but *Miracle on 34th Street* established the Irish redhead as an American favorite. One of her abiding memories of the movie was the close relationship she formed with her on-screen daughter, Natalie Wood.

At the tender age of nine, Natalie Wood already had five films to her credit before playing Susan Walker, the little girl who believes Kris Kringle really is Santa Claus.

What?

There have been several versions of *Miracle on 34th Street*, including one in 1994, in which Richard Attenborough played Santa.

The movie tells of Kris Kringle, an elderly, white-haired, bearded gentleman living in a nursing home. He discovers the man playing Santa Claus in the Macy's parade is drunk, and the event's organizer, Doris Walker, asks Kris to replace him. Doris's daughter, Susan, is delighted to meet Santa. Her cynical, world-weary mom asks Kringle to tell her daughter he isn't really Santa. But Kringle insists he is!

His insistence leads to a court case in which Santa has to prove his existence. The dreams of a little girl depend on it!

Where?

The story grew in Valentine Davies's imagination while he served in the Coast Guard during World War II. And New York City, where the film is set, was his hometown.

Thirty-fourth Street is the home of Macy's department store, and it is just before the Macy's Thanksgiving Day Parade, held between Seventy-seventh Street and Thirty-fourth Street, that Kris Kringle discovers the department store's hired Santa is worse the wear for drink!

In the 1994 remake starring Richard Attenborough, the store's name was changed to Cole's, although the Thirty-fourth Street location remained the same.

The trial that proves that Santa Claus really does exist takes place in the New York Supreme Court.

When?

The original *Miracle on 34th Street* was released in 1947—in the summer! The studio decided more people went to the movies in the summer than at Christmas. The posters featured Maureen O'Hara and John Payne and a distinct lack of anything Christmassy.

Previews showed studio executives trying to decide how to pitch this wonderful film to the public. Through a series of "chance" encounters with real-life film stars, they come to the conclusion that the movie has everything and will appeal to everyone. The words blazoned across the screen declare it to be "Hilarious! Romantic! Delightful! Charming! Tender! Exciting! Yes, and groovy! No kidding. . .it's a good picture!"

Why?

Valentine Davies had achieved some success as a screenwriter before World War II. He developed the story for *Miracle on 34th Street* during the hostilities and pitched it after the war. He wrote it up as a novel as it was being adapted into a screenplay.

Davies had two children and like most parents

would undoubtedly have had to answer the question "Does Santa Claus really exist?" His story helped answer that question for parents ever since!

Perhaps Davies had heard of the time in "Olde England" when Father Christmas was put "on tryall for inciting good people to drunkenness, gluttony, gaming and other licentious behaviour." He was acquitted of all charges!

24
Mistletoe

Who?

The Celts of prehistoric Europe were perhaps the first to find a use for mistletoe, although their uses were more practical than romantic. Pliny the Elder, the Roman philosopher and naturalist, wrote that the Celts used the plants as an antidote to poison and to increase the fertility of their cattle.

Mistletoe also featured in Scandinavian mythology, being the one living thing that could be used to kill the god Baldur, the son of Odin and brother of Thor. Baldur was so loved by everyone (except his slayer, his half-brother Loki) that the mistletoe's leaves hang their heads and weep because of their part in his death.

What?

Mistletoe is a parasitic plant that grows on, and out of, a variety of trees. Birds eat the plant and then drop the seeds on the branches of other trees. The seeds stick to the branches and grow there.

The growth of the mistletoe does affect the host plant, and too much mistletoe can kill a tree, but this particular parasite has been granted a special dispensation.

Mistletoe has been classified as an "ecological keystone species," meaning that an inordinate number of plants or creatures depend on it or benefit from it. Thanks to its association with Christmas decoration, it has also acquired a degree of cultural importance.

Where?

Mistletoe (*Viscus album*) once grew wild all across northern Europe, but these days it is mainly grown commercially for the Christmas market. It seems to prefer apple trees as a host.

Viscus album does not grow naturally in North America, but "Eastern" Mistletoe does. The only differences the casual observer would notice are that Eastern Mistletoe has shorter leaves and more berries.

As for where the mistletoe should be hung amidst the Christmas decorations, well, doorways seem to be a favorite place, and there is always a good chance of a man and woman meeting there, but it really depends on who has the mistletoe and whom they wish to kiss.

When?

The uses of mistletoe date back to the days when people lived more closely with nature and depended on wild plants more than we do now. It would undoubtedly have been noticed and thought special when the leaves fell from the trees in the fall but the mistletoe stayed green.

Pliny the Elder recorded its medicinal use among the Celts in the first century AD, but it had undoubtedly been used for centuries before that.

Washington Irving wrote about the tradition of kissing under the mistletoe in 1802.

Mistletoe should be hung with the rest of the Christmas decorations and taken down when the other decorations are taken down.

Why?

The ancient Celts used the evergreen plant to increase fertility in livestock and neutralize poisons in humans, despite the fact that eating it raw would make most people very sick.

These days it is still an ingredient in some homeopathic medicines, but the most common use for mistletoe involves claiming kisses at Christmas!

In Washington Irving's *The Sketch Book of Geoffrey Crayon*, he states that a man may claim a kiss if he catches a woman standing under the mistletoe. According to Irving, the man should pluck a berry from the sprig each time he claims a kiss. When the berries run out, so do his kissing privileges!

25

NORAD Tracking Santa

Who?

The North American Aerospace Defense Command (NORAD) is a joint initiative set up by the governments of Canada and the United States in anticipation of a possible Soviet nuclear missile strike during the Cold War. The shortest and quickest route for these missiles would have been across the North Pole and over Canada. Presumably Santa would have been the first to spot them, which makes it all the more ironic and appropriate that NORAD technology is now used to track Santa himself.

Colonel Harry Shoup was the right man in the right place when an unusual call to his command center gave him the chance to create a modern Christmas tradition.

What?

Each year NORAD keeps children the world over updated on Santa Claus's epic journey around the world. A team of volunteers (taking the place of the original military personnel) have staffed phone lines, produced newspaper stories, recorded messages, and answered e-mails. Corporate sponsorships cover the costs.

These days NORAD Tracks Santa has a strong online presence (www.noradsanta.org) and features on various social media platforms. Those children (of all ages) with Internet access can now log on and see "real-time" footage of Santa flying his sleigh past well-known landmarks in cities all around the world. Sometimes Santa even takes the time to wave at the camera!

Where?

Well, the tracking is done by NORAD, whose headquarters are in Colorado Springs. But the journey itself covers every country in the world. All in a single night! Once Santa has completed his mission of joy, NORAD advises viewers, "Santa has completed his flight this year. Come back next December to see him fly again!"

While the first "operators" to answer the phone were USAF personnel, we needn't worry about defense budgets being spent on the project these days. Various companies sponsor the operation, and a large team of dedicated friends of Santa Claus sit by the phones and operate the necessary technology on a voluntary basis.

When?

In 1955 a store advertised a phone number that they promised would get children through to Santa Claus. But someone somewhere in the advertising process made a mistake and published the number of CONAD, the Continental Air Defense Command (which became NORAD three years later).

The Santa-tracker program, which began in an unofficial way on that day, has continued, using various technologies.

As December begins, the NORAD Santa tracker begins a countdown to Christmas. On Christmas Eve the site updates each hour as midnight moves around the world.

Colonel Harry Shoup, USAF, affectionately known as "the Santa Colonel," passed away in 2009, at age ninety-two.

Why?

It was an accident! It might have ended before it began if it hadn't been for the good heart of the man in command on that day. When children started calling CONAD expecting to speak to Santa, Colonel Harry Shoup told his staff to give the children updates on how Santa was doing.

Why did they want to know? Well, children get excited about a visit from Santa. Just as on long journeys they will ask, "Are we there yet?" they want to know if Santa is almost here yet.

Lessons in geography and fraternity might also be gleaned from watching Santa visit *every* country in the world.

26

Poinsettias

Who?

Joel Roberts Poinsett was the U.S. Minister to Mexico from 1825 to 1830 and introduced the flower to the States in 1825. A botanist as well as a statesman, his name was attached to the poinsettia after he brought plants to the United States.

If one name has a greater connection to the flower than Poinsett's, it would be Ecke. German immigrant Albert Ecke sold them from a street stall. His son developed a better way of growing them, and soon the family supplied every poinsettia sold in the States. Even now the Ecke family provides half the poinsettias sold in the States and almost three-quarters of those sold worldwide.

What?

Legend tells of a girl in sixteenth-century Mexico who wanted to add something to her village church's Christmas display. But, poor as she was, she had nothing to give. An angel in disguise encouraged her to pick some roadside flowers—

which she thought were simply weeds! But she picked them, and she took the "weeds" to the church, where she laid them on the altar in a spirit of love.

Miraculously, the "weeds" flowered on the altar.

Poinsettias are now prominent in the decoration of churches of many denominations at Christmastime. Easy to keep as well as beautiful, they also decorate countless homes and workplaces over the festive season.

Where?

The poinsettia grew naturally in Mexico and in many parts of Central America. When the Ecke family had their virtual monopoly, the flowers were mostly grown in California.

Countries with similar environmental conditions to Mexico, like parts of Egypt and Australia, have also successfully cultivated the poinsettia. In Egypt it is known as *Bent el Consul,* or the consul's daughter, as a token of respect to Joel Poinsett.

Since the secret of growing poinsettias the Ecke way has become known outside the family, poinsettia production has increasingly moved back south of the border.

Poinsettias are now sold all across the world, especially in the lead-up to Christmastime.

When?

Despite being known as a Christmas flower, the poinsettia actually has a day of its own dedicated to it. Poinsettia Day is the twelfth of December, the birthday of Joel Roberts Poinsett.

The poinsettia is a "short day" flower. They flower best at the times of year when there are fewer than twelve hours of daylight in a day. In this way they are almost guaranteed the undivided attention of the pollinating insects, which have a much wider range of flowers at other times of the year.

Poinsettias were used for medicines and dyes by the Aztecs since at least as far back as the fourteenth century.

Why?

Of course, the poinsettias that poor Mexican girl brought would have flowered anyway, but the point is made that everything in God's creation is a miracle if seen the right way, even weeds. And Jesus doesn't want expensive offerings as birthday presents. He will accept the least little thing from even the poorest of us, if it is offered in a spirit of love.

The shape of the poinsettia leaves are said to imitate the Star of Bethlehem, and the deep-red color supposedly represents the blood Christ spilled for us at the Crucifixion. Thus one little flower symbolizes the birth and death of the Messiah.

27

Rudolph, the Red-Nosed Reindeer

Who?

Despite being the most famous of Santa's reindeer now, Rudolph was not always so well known. Robert Lewis May, a copywriter, wrote the reindeer's story down in a book meant to be given away free as a Christmas promotion.

Robert Lewis May's brother-in-law Johnny Marks was a songwriter with a special talent for writing Christmas songs. He took May's story and turned it into one of the most successful Christmas songs ever.

The "singing cowboy" Gene Autry had his biggest ever chart hit when "Rudolph the Red-nosed Reindeer" took him to number one in the music charts.

Rudolph himself is, of course, Santa's ninth and leading reindeer!

What?

Rudolph is a reindeer, but a very special one! Not

many people knew that flying reindeer pulled Santa's sleigh until Clement Clarke Moore let the secret out in his 1823 poem "'Twas the Night before Christmas."

While "ordinary" flying reindeer are quite capable of pulling a sleigh loaded with toys all around the world, they struggle a little in foggy weather—especially when the fog is so thick that Santa can't even see the reindeer at the front of his team.

Thankfully Rudolph has a nose that glows in the dark! This peculiar feature, which used to get him teased, proved to be just what Santa needed. Now Rudolph leads his team!

Where?

Reindeer, also known as caribou, are found around the world in arctic and subarctic environs. In some countries, because of climate change and population expansion, reindeer are finding it harder to survive these days. But in Santa's North Pole compound the reindeer are as happy as ever.

Robert Lewis May, who put Rudolph's story into print for the first time, lived in Illinois. His brother-in-law Johnny Marks, who wrote the song that took Rudolph into the music charts, was a New York City–based songwriter. He had a fondness for Christmas songs and also wrote another song about our favorite reindeer, "Run Rudolph Run," which was recorded by Chuck Berry.

When?
Rudolph's story first appeared in print (in poetic form) in 1939. That first Christmas the Montgomery Ward chain gave away 2.5 million free copies, which would have made a lot of children very happy!

After the end of World War II, publishing houses looked to cash in on the story's popularity and offered to buy the tale from Montgomery Ward. In 1947 the chairman of Montgomery Ward generously returned the copyright to Robert Lewis May, and the book was then published and made available to everyone.

The Gene Autry recording of the song based on the book was the first number-one song of the 1950s.

Why?
Rudolph never went in search of fame! Robert Lewis May was working for the department store and mail-order organization Montgomery Ward. They had a tradition of giving away coloring books to their customers' children at Christmastime. But it cost more money than they liked to spend

to buy these books. So they asked May to come up with a story so they could produce their own books. May must have heard about Rudolph and decided to write his story. The book was a huge success and is still in print today.

Rudolph does his continuing good work for the love of Santa and love of the world's children.

28
Santa Claus

Who?

Santa Claus, as everyone should know, is a kindly old gentleman who lives at the North Pole with his herd of reindeer and his elf friends. They spend the year making toys for good little children and getting ready for Christmas Eve.

On Christmas Eve the elves and Mrs. Claus wave good-bye to Santa as he and his reindeer begin their epic journey around the world. They visit every house in the world where little children live (including several houses where the "children" are quite a bit older) and leave gifts.

A "stout" gentleman, he has the surprising ability to get into some houses by dropping down their chimney!

What?

Santa Claus has seen many incarnations, and even today he appears in different guises. Since pre-Christian times he has been depicted as an elderly, white-bearded paternal figure, often larger in stature than the modern Santa. He would bring gifts and cheer at a time of year (in northern Europe at least) when the land was frozen and food was hard to come by. He may also have been an embodiment of the promise of spring, being dressed in green as he often was.

In modern times Santa has refined and developed his business until he has become a worldwide operation, visiting children everywhere.

Where?

In pre-Christian northern Europe, Odin was the bearded father figure said to fly across the sky in a great hunt. His image was later mixed with that of Saint Nicholas, a bishop in Asia Minor.

In England Father Christmas was the mid-winter cheer bringer, although his robes were green and he wore wreaths of laurel or holly in his hair.

The Dutch took *Sinterklass* (Saint Nicholas) to America with them, and America gave the world the modern interpretation of Santa Claus when Clement Clarke Moore, who lived in Troy, New York, described him as a fur-dressed, round-bellied, "jolly old elf" in his much-loved poem " 'Twas the Night before Christmas."

When?

When Christianity reached Europe, it began the tradition of Saint Nicholas, who was famous for giving presents (sometimes left in stockings) and who probably also had a long, white beard. His red robes may have influenced later depictions of Santa.

In the 1600s the English had the tradition of Father Christmas.

In 1825 a book called *A New-Year's Present to the Little Ones from Five to Twelve* mentioned a character called "Old Santeclaus" who apparently rode a sleigh and left anonymous gifts.

Our modern ideas of Santa Claus were formed, in large part, by the 1823 poem "A Visit from Saint Nicholas," better known now as " 'Twas the Night before Christmas."

Why?

In the agricultural communities of northern Europe, midwinter must have been a very quiet time—except for the midwinter festivals. Families would travel to be together, and, of course, they brought gifts. Children received presents from relatives who were busy working the rest of the year.

When Christianity arrived, with its idea of Christ as a gift to the world and Him being presented with gifts from Wise Men who had traveled "from afar," it must all have seemed so very familiar and right.

Santa Claus is a beautiful mix of Christian and pre-Christian traditions, and as such, he brings a lot of joy to a lot of children!

29
Secret Santa

Who?

There are countless Secret Santas each year during the festive period; individuals helping others anonymously in the finest traditions of Christmas. Every once in a while one of them will come to the attention of the wider world—like Larry Stewart. Stewart is estimated to have given away $1.3 million. Dressed in white dungarees, red shirt, and red hat, Stewart personally handed out hundred-dollar bills to people in need over a twenty-five-year period.

Before he died, in 2007, he trained other Secret Santas to follow in his footsteps.

Stewart eventually, reluctantly, made the headlines, but often the best work done each Christmas is done by really secret Santas!

What?

A Secret Santa is one who follows in the footsteps of the first Santa Claus, Saint Nicholas. He sneaked into a house at night to leave his gifts anonymously (starting the tradition that Santa comes down the chimney). Secret Santas also work in the spirit of the Sermon on the Mount. Jesus said, "But when thou doest alms, let not thy left hand know what thy right hand doeth: that thine alms may be in secret" (Matthew 6:3–4).

The Secret Santa idea may have begun as a convenient solution to a workplace problem, but it actually taps into the very best traditions of the season.

Where?

Most Secret Santas happen in the workplace. Rather than each person feeling obligated to buy individual gifts for all of their colleagues, everyone's name is put into a box or a bowl; then each person draws out one name at random. The Secret Santa buys a gift for that person, usually without indicating who it came from. There is often a price limit put on the gifts, and the pleasure comes more from the sense of camaraderie and mutual silliness than the gift itself.

Larry Stewart did most of his good work in Kansas City, but Secret Santas are at work everywhere—secretly!

When?

The first Santa to carry his work out in secret was Saint Nicholas, who did his good works in the early fourth century AD.

The act of kindness that inspired Larry Stewart's years of Secret Santa work happened in 1979, when Ted Horn "found" a twenty-dollar bill on the floor of a Dixie Diner and handed it to him, saying he must have dropped it (knowing that he hadn't!).

Stewart went from being penniless to making his fortune and paid that kind deed back many, many times over.

Workplace Secret Santas usually begin in early December, giving people time to shop and give their gifts before the Christmas holidays.

Why?

Larry Stewart began his philanthropic work after he had been broke and unable to pay for a meal. The owner of the diner pretended to find a twenty-dollar bill and gave it to him. In better times Stewart followed that example in giving his cash directly to people who needed it.

People like Stewart, who help others anonymously, are often appreciative of the blessings in their lives and want to share what they can with others who are less fortunate. For them the thanks aren't the important thing. They get that most underestimated of feelings, the pure pleasure of simply giving. If you don't know that pleasure, try being a Secret Santa!

30
"Silent Night"

Who?

Josef Franz Mohr's life got off to a terrible start. His parents were unmarried, and his father was an army deserter. Society would have wanted nothing to do with him. But choirmaster Johann Heirnle spotted his musical talent and sponsored him in his studies for the priesthood. While serving as a priest, Father Mohr wrote a poem entitled "Silent Night, Holy Night."

During a period of recuperation from illness, he met Franz Xaver Gruber, who put the poem to music. Herr Gruber was the local schoolmaster and church organist.

Later Father Mohr would recall his meeting with Herr Gruber as one of the most precious moments of his life.

What?

"Stille Nacht, Heilige Nacht," as it is called in the original German, was a song composed with a guitar accompaniment in mind, but it is just as beautiful with a full orchestral backing or no accompaniment at all.

While the modern version is contemplative, almost a lullaby, the original arrangement was a bit more upbeat.

The singing of "Silent Night" by soldiers led to Christmas truces in the Franco-Prussian war of 1870 and in the trenches in France during the First World War.

The song has been translated into at least forty-four languages, and Bing Crosby's version of the Christmas classic has sold more than ten million copies.

Where?

Joseph Mohr's first assignment as an assistant priest was in the Austrian village of Mariapfarr in the Salzburg district. Mariapfarr is where he is believed to have composed the poem "Stille Nacht, Heilige Nacht."

After falling ill, the priest was sent to recuperate in Salzburg. On his way to complete recovery, he was assigned to the Saint Nicholas Church in Oberndorf.

Franz Gruber was the schoolmaster at a nearby village and the organist at Saint Nicholas.

One day Mohr visited Gruber in his hometown

of Arnsdorf. The Gruber residence was where the words and music for what would become one of the most famous Christmas songs ever came together.

When?

Joseph Mohr was born in 1792. The lyrics to "Silent Night" were written around 1816, when Mohr would have been around twenty-four years old. The date when the music was added to the words is stated with uncommon certainty, Christmas Eve, 1818. That same evening, it was performed for the first time, in the Saint Nicholas Church in Oberndorf.

In 1859 John Freeman Young, who would shortly afterward become a bishop of the Episcopal Church, in Florida, gave the world the English translation most used today.

In 1943 Hertha Pauli, an Austrian displaced by World War II, wrote *Silent Night: A Story of a Song* for her young American readers.

Why?

There are many stories about why Father Mohr wrote "Silent Night." Most involve something terrible happening to the church organ just before the Christmas Eve service and the desperate priest having to come up with a hymn that could be sung without accompaniment. In some versions the church mice are responsible, having eaten the organ bellows!

In fact Father Mohr wrote his lyrics long before then, and church records show no such organ failure.

None of this takes away from the beauty of the song. And Gruber's achievement in putting a tune to the lyrics on the day it was to be performed was surely a minor miracle in its own right!

31

Star of Bethlehem

Who?

The Star of Bethlehem was the astronomical phenomenon that alerted the Magi, who lived somewhere in the east, that the Messiah was to be born. The Magi were either Wise Men, astronomers, kings, or all three. Their identity is never stated, but it is suggested in some traditions that they had been preparing for the coming of the King of the Jews for some time.

The Magi may have been responsible for the tradition of giving gifts at Christmas. The fact that they gave three gifts often leads people to assume there were three Magi, but this is never stated, and in some eastern cultures it is believed there were twelve.

What?

There are many theories as to what the Star of Bethlehem might have been. Astronomers have reverse-plotted the course of the planets to see if any of them might have been "in conjunction" at the right time.

Halley's Comet was in the sky—but not for a few years after the event. Chinese astronomers mention a large comet that appeared to hang in the sky for seventy days around the year 5 BC.

God could easily have aligned the planets or sent a comet to mark the birth of His son, but the star might also have been the light of the Lord shining down from on high.

Where?

If the Magi were in the east, the Star of Bethlehem must have risen in the west. This would have given them a direction but would not have helped pinpoint a destination.

After they talked to Herod, the star, which they had seen when it rose, appeared to take on a different role. It now traveled before them, leading them the few miles from Jerusalem to Bethlehem. A star hanging in the sky would have been of no use for that part of the journey, lending credence to the theory that the star was, in fact, a manifestation of God's power, a light sent to guide the Magi to a specific place.

When?

The Star of Bethlehem "rose" in the sky when

Jesus was born. When the Magi came to the court of King Herod, he carefully asked them when the star had appeared; then he ordered the killing of all boys in the Bethlehem area who were two years old or under. This suggests that the Magi had been traveling (or preparing and traveling) for two years. To have traveled such a distance suggests that the Magi had been anticipating the event for some time.

Astronomers have tried to connect the Star of Bethlehem with various astronomical events in the years around Christ's birth, but none of these attempts have been conclusive.

Why?

Jesus is predicted all through the Old Testament, so it is not unlikely that eastern Wise Men, or philosophers, might have read similar predictions in their own lands and looked forward to the sign in the heavens that would mark his arrival in this world.

By bringing the Wise Men to the manger, the Star of Bethlehem may have fulfilled the line in Isaiah that says, "Kings shall see and arise, princes also shall worship" (Isaiah 49:7).

Perhaps it is not inappropriate that the birth of one who would become known as "the Light of the World" should be marked by a guiding light in the darkness.

32

"The Christmas Song"

Who?

"The Christmas Song" was written by Mel Torme and Bob Wells. Torme was a singer whose voice was described as being like velvet fog. He was also a composer, author, and actor. Wells was a songwriter, scriptwriter, and television producer. Torme recorded the song several times, but it will forever be associated with Nat King Cole, who recorded the song at least four times. Cole was Mel Torme's first choice for the song.

Most people who have ever recorded a Christmas album have included "The Christmas Song." There have been at least ninety covers by well-known artists such as Garth Brooks, James Brown, Rosemary Clooney, Celine Dion, and Bob Dylan.

What?

"The Christmas Song" is probably better known by its first line, "Chestnuts roasting on an open fire." It was originally entitled "Merry Christmas to You." Perhaps its writers felt it might be a little presumptuous to call their creation "*The* Christmas Song," but the end result has as good a claim to that title as any other. If, of course, we are only talking about secular songs! "The Christmas Song" has no spiritual content but plenty of nostalgia and warm feeling.

Add Nat King Cole's velvety voice to that mix, and you have a song that is as much a Christmas treat as any rich, chocolaty, sugar-laden dessert.

Where?

"The Christmas Song" was written on a scorchingly hot day near Toluca Lake in the San Fernando Valley. Mel Torme arrived at Bob Wells's house for a prearranged work session. Torme let himself in, and Wells, who had been suffering in the heat, was nowhere to be seen. His notes, an attempt to write himself cool, were sitting on a music board. Torme saw them and recognized a hit in the making. Forty-five minutes after Wells came into the room, they had the song completed.

The Nat King Cole Trio recorded the song for the first time in WMCA Radio Studios in New York City.

When?

The collaboration, one of many between Mel Torme and Bob Wells, came about in July 1944.

Despite Nat King Cole loving the song and his being Torme's first choice as singer, he was so busy it took almost two years for him to get around to recording it. He recorded it for the first time in June 1946, then again a month later, then again in 1952, and for the last time (and for the first time in stereo) in 1961.

The original King Cole Trio recording was inducted into the Grammy Hall of Fame in 1974.

Mel Torme recorded the song in 1954, 1961, 1966, and 1992.

Why?

Bob Wells wasn't enjoying the heat. Pacing his house in tennis shorts and a polo shirt, he decided to try to write something cooling. "All I could think about was Christmas and cold weather," he told Mel Torme.

The notes he scribbled down were, "Chestnuts roasting on an open fire. Jack Frost nipping at your nose. Yuletide carols being sung by a choir. And folks dressed up like Eskimos."

That afternoon Torme and Wells completed something that would go on to become possibly the most-performed Christmas song ever.

By immersing themselves in winter, in the middle of summer, Wells and Torme made Christmas a little cozier for everyone.

33

The National Christmas Tree

Who?

Frederick Morris Feiker, who was press aide to Herbert Hoover while Hoover was the secretary of commerce, came up with the idea of a National Christmas Tree. Calvin Coolidge was the president Feiker had to convince. The first lady, Grace Coolidge, chose the location. The Electric League of Washington donated the twenty-five hundred red, white, and blue bulbs that adorned the tree, while the tree itself was donated by Middlebury College in Vermont.

The first family was joined by three thousand schoolchildren and six thousand residents of Washington for a carol service after the tree was lit. The gathering was segregated on racial lines with African Americans being allowed in after midnight.

What?

The National Christmas Tree (or the National Community Christmas Tree, as it was called in early days) has been many different types of trees over the years. It has been a live tree, a planted tree, a cut tree, and at times there have been two of them alternating. It has never been an artificial tree. It has been a balsam fir, a Norway spruce, a blue spruce, a red cedar, an Oriental spruce, and, as of 2011, it has been a Colorado blue spruce.

The trees have brought pleasure to millions of Christmas visitors, but they have suffered from environmental conditions, heat damage from the Christmas lights, and even train derailments!

Where?

The first National Christmas Tree was placed in the Ellipse outside the White House, the site approved by Grace Coolidge. The next tree was planted on the west side of Sherman Plaza. On other years, it has been situated in Lafayette Park, to the north of the White House, the South Lawn, and in various other sites around the White House grounds.

Some of these location shifts were made to give a more "homey" appearance, some to allow more people to have access, some for better TV coverage, and some were for security reasons.

Eventually the tree moved back to its original home in the northeast quadrant of the Ellipse.

When?

The first ever National Christmas Tree was erected on the Ellipse in time for Christmas, 1923. In

1924, after President Coolidge criticized the cutting down of so many trees for Christmas, a live tree was transplanted to Washington for the occasion.

In 1927 President Coolidge addressed the crowd before switching on the lights, a tradition that most presidents have followed since then.

The first year that decorations other than lights were put on the tree was 1929. In 1933 speakers hidden in the branches of the tree played Christmas music, and the notion of the "Singing Tree" was born.

In 1946 the lighting ceremony was televised for the first time.

Why?

The first electrical Christmas tree lights had been lit in 1882, but even forty years later they were still seen as a novelty too expensive for the average household. Electricity companies were forever looking for ways to encourage people to use more electricity and electrical appliances. There was even a Society for Electrical Development.

Frederick Morris Feiker was an electrical engineer and writer for the industry, as well as a press officer for the Department of Commerce. He thought that if the White House lit a Christmas tree with electricity (lights, cables, and power supplied free by the electricity companies) that the idea might catch on. It did!

34

" 'Twas the Night before Christmas"

Who?

Because the poem "A Visit from St. Nicholas" first appeared in print with no name attached, the authorship has since been disputed. The generally accredited author is Clement Clarke Moore, a professor at the General Theological Seminary in Manhattan and author of several scholarly works.

Fellow New Yorker and poet Henry Livingston, Jr., was the other candidate. The poem appeared in print for the first time five years before his death. Livingston's children would later claim they remembered their father reading them the poem as early as 1807, sixteen years before its first anonymous publication. They believed it had been written by him.

What?

In 1999 the authors of *A History of New York City to 1898* referred to "A Visit from St. Nicholas" as "arguably the best known verses ever written by an American." Not so well recognized under its original title these days, most people know it by these words from its first line, " 'Twas the Night before Christmas."

The poem made popular the idea of Santa Claus (although he is referred to here only as Saint Nicholas) as a visitor bearing toys and other gifts on Christmas Eve. It portrayed him as a jolly old elf, and for perhaps the first time in print, gave us the names of Santa's reindeer.

Where?

"A Visit from St. Nicholas" first appeared in print in the *Troy* (New York) *Sentinel*. Though the newspaper had a poetry section, the proprietors seemed to think this anonymous submission was worthy of a separate location. They described it as having "a spirit of cordial goodness in it, a playfulness of fancy, and a benevolent alacrity to enter into the feelings and promote the simple pleasures of children, which are altogether charming," and recommended it to their "little patrons, both lads and lasses."

The staff of the *Troy Sentinel* made the connection between St. Nicholas and the "delightful personification of parental kindness" they called "Santa Claus."

When?

Believe it or not, between churches, there was some

dispute at the time as to when was the best time to hold the major family celebration, on Christmas Day or New Year's Day. In placing his poem on the night before Christmas, Moore managed to sidestep the disputed twenty-fifth and, at the same time, reinforce its preeminence.

"A Visit from St. Nicholas" was published anonymously two days before Christmas Day, 1823. It took until 1844 for Moore to include it in a collection of his works.

The poem has never gone out of fashion, having been reprinted, referred to, and spoofed in publications, radio shows, TV, and films ever since.

Why?

Despite there being some doubt over who really wrote "A Visit from St. Nicholas," both main contenders for the honor would more than likely have written it for the same reason. As the poem went unclaimed for quite some time, it is unlikely that it was written for acclaim or for money.

Clement Clarke Moore was a serious Bible scholar; Henry Livingston, Jr., was a soldier, farmer, and poet—but both were fathers, and the true author undoubtedly intended the verses as fun and entertainment for his children.

It has been read in the same spirit by parents to children ever since those days!

35

The Twelve Days of Christmas

Who?

The twelve days of Christmas are about Jesus. They begin on the supposed day of His birth and end on the day He is traditionally thought to have been presented to the world.

In times gone by there would have been a church service on each of the Twelve Days, but because families would come together for these services and very little work was being done anyway, it gradually became more about celebration than adoration.

The practice of giving a gift on each of those days would, of necessity, have been more prevalent among the wealthier classes of society (although humble gifts given with love would have been very suitable).

What?

The original twelve days of Christmas were (and are) the period of celebration between Christmas

Day and Epiphany. In some cultures gifts are exchanged on December 25, in others on the last day of the period. In times gone by it was also common to give a gift on each of the twelve days—just as in the song!

In our more secular world, these days, the twelfth day after Christmas is simply the time we usually take down the decorations.

In earlier times Twelfth Night, at the end of the twelve days, was the major celebration. Today, Christmas Day, the first of the twelve, dominates the period.

Where?

The Twelve Days are a period of worship almost as old as the church itself. It spread east and west with the different traditions of the church. It became firmly established as a time of revelry in medieval England. So much so that William Shakespeare preserved it in his play *Twelfth Night*. From England the celebration of twelve days spread across the British Empire.

Although the custom is declining in popularity, many churches in the United States still celebrate the Twelve Days either by giving gifts on each of the days or lighting a candle for each day.

Wherever Christmas is celebrated, there will,

in one form or another, be the Twelve Days of Christmas.

When?

The Twelve Days of Christmas begin on December 25 and run up until Twelfth Night, on the evening of January 5.

Thanks to a medieval custom, Twelfth Day actually follows Twelfth Night and is held on January 6. Twelfth Night (where it is still celebrated) is usually an evening of festivities marking the end of a time of adoration and gift-giving.

In medieval times Twelfth Night was actually the end of a winter festival that began at Halloween!

The carol "The Twelve Days of Christmas" was first published in 1780, although it is undoubtedly much older. It describes the tradition of giving a gift on each of the days.

Why?

The Christian church sees the birth of Jesus Christ and His presentation to the world, known as Epiphany, as the first two major events in His life. The twelve days between the two feast days became an extended period of thanksgiving.

The western churches regard Epiphany as the day He was adored by the Magi, thus presenting himself to the Gentiles. Jesus would have been under two years old, no longer a newborn baby.

The eastern churches see it as the day He was baptized and proclaimed the Son of God for all to see and hear. In this interpretation the twelve days cover thirty years of his life.

36
Wassailing

Who?

Wassailing is an old northern European tradition that was happily adopted by the English. Farmers and other orchard owners saw a pre-Christian ceremony of incantations and songs sung to their trees either as something that would ensure a good crop the next year or as a good excuse to drink to excess in the middle of winter.

A more popular variant of the tradition has farm laborers and villagers singing outside the local landowner's home in the hope that their wishes of good luck would bring forth good food and hot spiced drinks. Several of the older wassailing songs specifically point out that the singers are not beggars but kindly neighbors wishing the hearers good health.

What?

Wassailing and caroling are not so very different these days. Perhaps the main difference is that wassailing tended to involve more drink being imbibed, usually in the form of mulled wine and other seasonal brews.

Wassailing basically involves singing songs of good cheer in exchange for food and drink, although in the south of England there is an ancient tradition of singing to the apple trees at Christmas to ensure a good crop the following year.

Popular wassailing songs include "Here We Come A-Wassailing," "The Wassailing Song," "We Wish You a Merry Christmas," and other carols that wish the listener good health or a good time.

Where?

While the tradition originated in mainland Europe, the English took to it with a real enthusiasm. Most of that country's apple orchards lie to the south, and many of the southern counties have wassailing songs specific to their area. Those apples would be used to make cider, and some of the previous year's cider would be spilled on the trees, as if to show them what was expected the next year.

A Romanian tradition that traveled to Britain involves the farmer threatening each tree with his ax. Then his wife comes along and kindly tells the tree that it will be okay—if it gives a good crop!

When?

The origins of wassailing are lost in the mists of time. When William the Conqueror invaded England in 1066, it was already a firmly established tradition.

The "official" wassailing night is Twelfth Night, but as Christmas rose to prominence, many of the Twelfth Night traditions moved backward. Now wassailers and carolers might go out at the same time (usually the week before Christmas). Indeed, they may be the same people singing the same songs!

Die-hard traditionalists might be tempted to go wassailing on January 17, although they might get some strange looks. This was the date of Twelfth Night before Western Europe adopted the Gregorian calendar.

Why?

The word *wassail* may be of Norse origin, or it might be of Anglo-Saxon derivation, but it became firmly entrenched in Old English as a way of wishing others "good health!" When not being shouted or sung to neighbors, the greeting was often offered to fruit trees to encourage them to greater fertility.

Whereas in olden times villagers might have gone wassailing in hope of food, drink, or even money, modern wassailers (while not averse to the food or the drink) might use the opportunity to raise money for good causes.

While specifically not a Christian tradition, wassailing's practice of enthusiastically wishing others good health is surely worthy of encouragement.

37

"White Christmas"

Who?

The song "White Christmas" was written by Irving Berlin, who also wrote "There's No Business Like Show Business," "Easter Parade," "God Bless America," and many other classics. Berlin is generally considered one of the greatest songwriters who ever lived. Composer Jerome Kern once said of him, "He has no place in American music—he is American music!"

Despite being sung by countless artists over the decades, "White Christmas" will forever be associated with that archetypal crooner Bing Crosby. Crosby famously downplayed his part in the song's success by saying it was so good a jackdaw with a cleft palate could have sung it and had a hit.

What?

"White Christmas" is an unashamed trip down Memory Lane to Christmases "just like the ones

I used to know." After he wrote it, Irving Berlin is said to have claimed he had just finished the best song he had ever written, then immediately amended it to the best song *anyone* had ever written.

The song went on to sell more copies than anyone can now count and is regularly reported as the biggest-selling song ever. So Berlin may well have been right in his assessment!

"White Christmas" was broadcast on armed forces radio during the Vietnam War as a pre-arranged signal that the evacuation of Saigon was beginning.

Where?

Popular legend has Irving Berlin writing "White Christmas" by a poolside in Phoenix, Arizona, not usually an area noted for much in the way of snowfall.

The song's first public outing was on a radio show, where it was sung by Bing Crosby. He sang it again in the Mark Sandrich movie *Holiday Inn* and again in the Michael Curtiz movie *White Christmas*.

It appeared on Bing Crosby's 1948 Christmas album, an album that has never been out of production since then. It's also featured on Christmas albums by Andy Williams, Doris Day,

Barbra Streisand, Elvis, Jim Reeves, Dean Martin, Dionne Warwick, Neil Sedaka, and many, many others.

When?

Irving Berlin wrote "White Christmas" in 1940. Its first radio outing took place on Christmas Day, 1941. *Holiday Inn*, which featured the song, was released in 1942. "White Christmas" won that year's Academy Award for the best original song. In the same year it topped the Billboard Chart and the Harlem Hit Parade. It was the Christmas Number One for Crosby in 1942, 1945, and 1946.

In 1954 the song appeared on the silver screen again when Crosby sang it in the movie named after the song, *White Christmas*.

In 2002 the Library of Congress included it in the National Recordings Registry as a song of cultural significance.

Why?

Irving Berlin was a prolific songwriter with an estimated fifteen hundred songs to his credit. An immigrant from Russia, he was fascinated by American culture, and it would have been strange indeed if one of his compositions had not featured the traditional American Christmas.

The combined talents of Berlin and Crosby ought to have been enough to guarantee the song's success. Adding a large dose of nostalgia at a time when the country was going to war and many would be separated from home and family seems to have made it into something of a phenomenon. It will probably be associated with Christmas as long as there *is* a Christmas.

38
Writing to Santa

Who?

Who writes to Santa Claus? Well, it is almost exclusively children who hope to get specific presents at Christmas. Of course, Santa is far too busy making toys to personally answer all those letters, but most major postal operations have teams of volunteers willing to help out with that.

Often the only answer a child gets is the toy itself.

The writer Mark Twain once presented his daughter with a letter written by Santa Claus, "also known as The Man in the Moon." Specific instructions were given on what she was to do to receive the presents Santa would be bringing from his base on the moon.

What?

Letters to Santa Claus can take many forms. Traditionally they were actual letters, often the very first letters a child would write. Sometimes they were posted, and sometimes they were burned. In this modern age it is perfectly acceptable for a child to e-mail Santa, although this may lack a little of the glamour of a real letter.

Failing writing materials or electronic devices, wishes or prayers are thought to work as well. Although, in the case of prayers, it is not certain whether God passes them on to Santa or Santa's helpers (the parents) overhear them from the other side of the bedroom door.

Where?

Wherever a child believes in Santa Claus, there needs to be a way to communicate with him. In many countries children would traditionally write their letters by the fireside, and then they would, very carefully, put their letters in the flames. The idea was that while the paper would burn away, the message would last and go up the chimney. Then the wind would blow it to the North Pole.

These days most children use the postal service.

No matter where the letters originate or which intermediate address is used, they generally end up at either Santa's base in Lapland or at his home at the North Pole.

When?

Amazingly most of the letters to Santa will have

been posted in the week before Christmas. In the case of letters burned in the fire, they will often be sent on Christmas Eve. Yet Santa, who has been making toys all year round, will still have the right toy for the right girl or boy. No one has yet explained how this can be so. It just is.

Answers to those letters, if they come via other organizations working for Santa, may take some time to be delivered. But the ultimate answer to any child's letter to Santa, the gift, will usually be delivered by Christmas Day morning.

Why?

How is Santa going to know what the child wants without a letter of some sort? Sure, the parents can suggest things, but what do they know? A letter from the child is sure to ask for the right thing.

Letter-writing is the perfect way to involve children in the wonder of that side of Christmas. They learn how to ask politely, be specific about what they want, and to add an appreciative thank you.

And if they think their behavior might have earned them a place on the naughty list, then a neat and polite letter might just change Santa's impression of them for the better.

39
Xmas

Who?

Christmas, or Xmas. It's all about Jesus!

It may also be about people who want to celebrate Christmas without any spiritual content, so they cross "Christ" out—but they are making a big mistake.

The first people to use the letter *X* for Christ were early Jews, either Hellenistic Jews or simply those who read Greek. *X*, or the Greek letter *chi* (which translates into English as *ch*), is the first part of the Greek word *Christos*, or "Christ." Sometimes *XP* was used, adding the Greek letter *rho* (the English *r*), the next letter in "Christos." This symbol is called the *Chi-Rho*.

The poet Samuel Coleridge; the writer Lewis Carroll (who was actually church deacon Charles Dodgson); and Oliver Wendell Holmes, Jr., the Supreme Court judge; all used the term Xmas at one time or another. They were probably not being disrespectful in the matter.

Prominent faith leaders have called for the word to be avoided.

What?

Every year people send or receive cards with the words "Merry Xmas" either written inside or printed on the front. A few will be making a point about a Christmas without faith, but most won't even have thought about it. For them it will just be a quick, convenient way of wishing someone a happy holiday. But for others it will be a thoughtless, perhaps offensive, way of crossing Christ out of Christmas.

While the usage of the term may have changed in the modern era, the term itself has a long history, going back to a time long before greeting cards were even invented.

Where?

According to popular legend, early Christians used *X* or *XP* as a code for Jesus, to help them avoid identification and persecution. Once Roman Emperor Constantine converted to Christianity, however, the symbol became much more mainstream, since a golden *XP* often topped his personal standard.

With that kind of backing, the symbol spread right across the empire and was even mentioned in *The Anglo-Saxon Chronicles* in the west. At no point was it intended as a replacement for the name of Jesus.

Today, shops and businesses may use it in their displays or promotional literature, but generally only for space-saving reasons.

When?

Since the first century, when people started writing about Jesus, they would refer to the Lord as *Christos* and use the abbreviations *X* or *XP*.

The term *Christmas* only really became popular in the Middle Ages, when it was spelled *Christemasse* or *Cristes maesse*.

In 1100 AD *The Anglo-Saxon Chronicle* used the term "Xpes maesse" for Christmas.

The Emperor Constantine adopted the *Chi-Rho* symbol in 312 AD, after his whole army had a vision from God.

So, Xmas is not a new invention. It has probably been used as long as the word *Christmas*, and using *X* for Jesus predates even that.

Why?

Is "Xmas" a cultural phenomenon? Is it deliberate snub? Is it thoughtless or accidental? It might be all of those things, but, traditionally, it has been used as a shortening of the word *Christmas* rather than any snub to the Man concerned.

But should we worry over its use? Could Jesus ever be crossed out? Of course not! Jesus doesn't live in a word; He is *the* Word! Neither can He be confined to one day, whether it be Christmas Day or Xmas Day. So let's worry less about "crossing Christ out of Christmas" and more about including Him in every other day of the year.

40

Yule Log

Who?

Father Christmas, a very big man according to English folklore, is often depicted carrying a Yule log on his shoulder.

In many cultures the eldest male of the house is sent, in his best clothes as a mark of respect, to chop down the tree selected that year. Other men will then be required, since, as tradition dictates, the Yule log should be carried home at shoulder height. The women of the house or the village play their part by decorating the felled tree with ribbons.

People visiting the house after the log is burning are encouraged to hit it and raise sparks for good luck.

What?

While some eastern European cultures use the Yule log as part of religious practices, the log itself has no real spiritual significance. It is simply a large log, preferably one of the harder woods, which will burn for a long time and keep a family or a village warm.

Sometimes whole trees were used as the Yule log. In houses with big enough rooms, the base of the tree would be fed into the fireplace and the log moved farther in as it burned.

In modern times families are more likely to have a chocolate cake representing a Yule log in their house than the real thing.

Where?

The Yule log is another tradition from the cold, dark northern European lands. The word *Yule* is an old Viking word for the midwinter celebrations.

While the tradition does come to America from the United Kingdom, there is evidence that it was popular with the Germanic peoples and the Slavs long before it ever came to the United Kingdom.

In Catalan homes, the Yule log was not burned. Instead it would be wrapped in a blanket and fed grass! When the time for presents arrived, the father of the house would beat the tree then take the blanket off it, exposing gifts that had apparently been expelled from the body of the tree.

When?

The Celtic peoples of Europe burned Yule logs for centuries before Christianity reached them. The tradition didn't change much afterward. The log is traditionally brought into the home on Christmas Eve and set alight. A good Yule log will be long enough and hard enough to keep burning throughout the Twelve Days of Christmas. For the sake of tradition, continuity, and good luck, the new Yule log should be lit with a piece of wood saved from the previous year's log.

Of course, the modern chocolate Yule logs are usually laid out for Christmas dinner and rarely last longer than the dinner itself!

Why?

In the short, cold days of midwinter, people dependant on the seasons for their survival must have occasionally wondered if the long, warm days of summer would ever return. Keeping a good fire, or a Yule log, burning was seen as a way of encouraging the sun to come back. More practically it was a good way of not freezing.

Keeping one fire burning throughout the Twelve Days of Christmas would have been conducive to long parties and a general air of merrymaking.

Where a religious meaning was looked for, it was suggested the burning log might symbolize keeping the Lord's stable warm between Christmas and Epiphany.

Also from author
David McLaughlan

HEAVEN—HERE AND NOW:
True Stories of God's Kingdom Here on Earth

If life is a test of sorts, a journey preparing us for heaven—shouldn't there be bits of heaven around us already? This book unveils them! In the book of Matthew, Jesus repeatedly describes heaven—and each time He uses ordinary, earthly examples. This world has many wonderful and mysterious aspects that we might think better suited to describe something as magnificent as heaven—but Jesus uses mustard seeds, hiring workers, children, and weeds as examples. Heaven—Here and Now considers those examples—chosen for a different culture in a different time—and applies them to the here and now, to the everyday stuff of our ordinary lives. It's a beautiful preview of heaven.

ISBN 978-1-61626-826-8
Paperback • 5.1875 x 8 • 224 pages

Available January 2013
wherever Christian books are sold

About the Author

David McLaughlan used to write whatever turned a buck, but now he writes about faith and God. It doesn't pay as well—but it does make his heart sing! He lives in bonnie Scotland with Julie and a whole "clan" of children.